33
INSPIRATIONAL
QUOTES

The comeback is always greater than the setback.

A smooth sea never made a skilled sailor.

Become better, not bitter.

I didn't come this far just to come this far.

Nobody cares—work harder.

Trust the process.

The devil whispered in my ear, "You can't withstand the storm."
I whispered back, "I am the storm."

One day at a time.

Nothing changes if nothing changes.

I work hard because I can't fuck up. I don't have anyone to fall back
on. I am the backup.

God gives his toughest battles to his strongest soldiers.

We turn our L's into lessons.

An obstacle is a brilliantly disguised opportunity.

You can't go back and change the beginning, but you can start where
you are and change the ending.

Discipline will take you places motivation can't.

Your current situation is not your final destination.

Throw me to a pack of wolves, and I shall return the leader of the pack.

You can't be bitter and expect life to be sweet.

I got tired of waiting for the light at the end of the tunnel and lit
that bitch up myself.

Tough times don't last, but tough people do.

We don't say, "Why me?" We say, "Try me."

Never give up.

When you see me with everything I deserve, just know I waited my turn.

Be a warrior, not a worrier.

I'm sorry my spirit irritates your demons.

You have been assigned this mountain to show others it can be moved.

A bitter root will only produce a bitter fruit.

Never let your emotions rule your intelligence.

Turned my mess into greatness.

If you deserve it, the universe will serve it.

Magic happens when you don't give up even though you want to.
The universe always falls in love with a stubborn heart.

I didn't get anything I prayed for until I became the type of person
who should receive it.

The best view comes from the hardest climb.

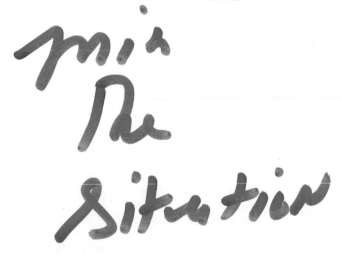

— MIKE "THE SITUATION" SORRENTINO
AUTHOR OF *REALITY CHECK*

HOW I OVERCAME ADDICTION, LOSS, AND PRISON
MIKE SORRENTINO
with Andy Symonds

REALITY CHECK
MAKING THE BEST OF THE SITUATION

Verified Publishing
an imprint of Ballast Books

Ballast Books, LLC
www.ballastbooks.com

Copyright © 2023 by Mike Sorrentino and Andy Symonds

ISBN: 978-1-955026-91-8

Printed in Hong Kong

Published by Ballast Books and Verified Publishing
www.ballastbooks.com | www.verifiedpublishing.com

For more information, bulk orders, appearances, or speaking requests, please email: info@ballastbooks.com

To my wife and kids, family and friends, and fans who never gave up on me.
The comeback is always greater than the setback.

TABLE OF CONTENTS

Prologue   1

Introduction   3

Chapter One
Meet The Situation   7

Chapter Two
Mis-Education   13

Chapter Three
Male Stripping   19

Chapter Four
The Love of My Life   23

Chapter Five
Drug Dealing   27

Chapter Six
A Relationship with the Devil   33

Chapter Seven
Rehab (#1)   43

Chapter Eight
The Situation Finds Inspiration   49

Chapter Nine
Green Lit   59

Chapter Ten
Welcome to the Shore   65

Chapter Eleven
Making a Show   71

Chapter Twelve
A Star Is Born   79

Chapter Thirteen
The Grip Gets Tighter   89

Chapter Fourteen
A Celeb to Celebrities   95

Chapter Fifteen
Situation, Inc.   103

Chapter Sixteen   109
Hitting a Wall

Chapter Seventeen   115
The Ultimatum

Chapter Eighteen   123
Rehab (#2)

Chapter Nineteen   129
Winter Is Coming

Chapter Twenty   135
Reconciliation and Loss

Chapter Twenty One   145
Another Chase and Another Rehab (#3)

Chapter Twenty Two   155
Rock Bottom

Chapter Twenty Three   163
Surrender and the Final Rehab

Chapter Twenty Four   173
Karma Returned

Chapter Twenty Five   179
Guilty

Chapter Twenty Six   187
A Reboot and a Proposal

Chapter Twenty Seven   195
The Sentence

Chapter Twenty Eight   201
"Take Me to Jail"

Chapter Twenty Nine   209
Welcome to Otisville

Chapter Thirty   219
A New Chapter

Chapter Thirty One   227
Dreams into Nightmares

Epilogue   235

PROLOGUE

Forewarning: What you're about to read is both shocking and mind-blowing. You will likely be astonished by many of the accounts told within. Sex, drugs, and reality stars, the stuff the cameras and tabloids never showed you. In some cases, I can barely believe these are my own stories. During the final editing process, as I reviewed these often unbelievable accounts of my life, I found myself feeling simply grateful and blessed to even be alive.

At its core, this is an inspirational story. One about never giving up, no matter how many times you've been knocked down. It's a story of redemption and positivity, or, as I like to say, "resilience in all its brilliance." This book details my experience, strength, and hope. My desire is for you to enjoy reading it as much as I enjoyed writing it. If you take away half of what I put into it, consider yourself as having come out ahead.

At the end of the day, I'm honored you decided to take this journey with me. Sincerely, from the bottom of my heart, thank you. Without my fans, there is no Situation. I always believed that one day I would detail to the world how I overcame so many trials and tribulations in the hope that it would become a part of someone else's survival guide. That's my goal for this book: to help as many people as possible by telling the story of Mike The Situation that no one knows.

Aside from the tabloid fodder—and yeah, there's a lot of that—this book is also a love story. A classic one at that: Boy meets girl. They fall in love. Boy loses girl. After much pain, boy gets girl back. If Shakespeare had been a reality star, he may have written this book.

I remain brutally honest and accountable throughout its duration. You will hear the sordid details of many of my unpredictable and outlandish adventures. I hold nothing back within these pages. I divulge the good, the bad, and the ugly. There's a lot of all three. That's my promise

1

to you, the reader—to keep everything true and honest, as it happened. But I'll also try to keep it light and positive because that's how I live my life. I've always been that way. To be honest, my personality is much like you see on TV. Just slightly less…extra.

During the throes of my drug addiction—most of which were played across your television screen even if you didn't know it at the time—I was my own worst enemy. It has always been me versus me. Battling my demons. In my younger years, I didn't know how to control those demons, and too often I lost the battles. But in the past eight years of sobriety, the tides have turned. I refuse to lose the war, though I still fight these battles every day.

Even as a now champion of addiction, I recognize that this is a lifetime fight against the monster lying dormant inside me. I'm fully aware that somewhere deep below, ever lurking, that darkness remains present. 'Tis the nature of life and this disease. I will never stop working to ensure that the old Sitch never claws his way out and rears his ugly head.

I win each day by exercising, maintaining a healthy lifestyle, focusing on mindful decision-making, and leaning on my faith. Each day is tackled one at a time, adhering to the principles of the twelve steps and having the acceptance that life is going to happen on life's terms. Every day, I practice being my best self and being better than the day before. Once each day is over, I place my head on the pillow, let go, and let God handle the rest.

But before all that, as a handsome young Italian American with a cocksure smile and a quick mouth, I was another carefree kid with big hopes and dreams. Unfortunately, after achieving those dreams, I subsequently let them slip through my fingers. It would take a journey through hell and back for me to climb that mountain once again. But I did make it and have decided to share it all with you here.

To quote Joe Rogan: "I love a success story, but even more than a success story, I like a dude-who-fucks-his-life-up-and-gets-his-life-together-again story."

I'd say that sums up The Situation pretty well.

INTRODUCTION

December 24, 2010
Howell, New Jersey

The comforting and familiar smell of Mom's baked clams filled the house; sautéing garlic, butter, and olive oil sizzled invitingly from the kitchen.

My brother Frank stood at the counter pouring large glasses of red wine. Melissa, our sister, set the gigolo bread and salad around the table. Shrimp, clams, and lobster, all oreganata, sat steaming on the counter in preparation for dinner to be called while Mom—Mama Peaches to all who loved her—put the final touches on her famous whole crab linguine with fra diavolo sauce that she'd been preparing since 6:00 a.m. The picked-over remnants of an antipasto platter and shrimp cocktail were pushed aside as everyone waited for the final dishes to be served. Christmas tree icicles blinked under muted lights as *The Godfather Part II* played on the TV. Christmas Eve dinner, Sorrentino style—my favorite meal of the year. The Feast of the Seven Fishes, and Mama Peaches did not hold back.

The whole family wore wide smiles. Not only was it Christmas, but the youngest son—previously the black sheep of the family—was suddenly world famous, rich, and the star of one of the biggest television shows in the world. It didn't get any better than this.

"Mike, we had a great year, but we still need to file a tax return." That was Marc, my other brother and manager, calling out to me like he had just remembered something important but not *that* important. Certainly not as important as the fried calamari coming off the stove; at least that's how I viewed his admonition at the time.

From my prone position on the couch, I rolled over and continued pecking at my brand-new iPhone 4 while simultaneously basking in my famousness. As always during those days, I was high as all hell on prescription opiates, though no one in my family could tell. The Situation was a pro at hiding—and feeding—his demons. Or at least I thought so.

Wait—did he just refer to himself in the third person? Who does that?

Yes. Yes, I did. And to answer your question, The Situation talks in third person, that's who. Is it ridiculous? It surely is. But at the same time, it's amazing. Because sometimes, ridiculous *is* amazing.

Anyway, Marc was right. It had been a great year, my first full one in entertainment. It was like I'd hit the lotto. The Situation was a household name and booming business. The reality show I starred in, *Jersey Shore*, had exploded into a cultural phenomenon. "DTF," "grenade," and "smushing" had all entered the American lexicon like heat-seeking missiles.

A couple months earlier, Leonardo DiCaprio had sought me out at the club—Coco de Ville in West Hollywood. He was there with Bar Refaeli, and when he saw me, he grinned wildly before dapping me up and yelling in my ear, "GTL all day!" President Obama mentioned me during his speech at that year's Correspondents' Association dinner, ironically joking that, "The Situation should be exempt from the tanning tax." (Hmmm. I wonder if this offer still stands and my accountants can apply for a tax credit. Unfortunately, years later, the government would not adhere to the president's guidance to go easy on my tax obligations.)

GQ magazine, which had just named me its "Sensation of the Year," estimated my earnings at five million dollars that year. I wasn't sure, but it sounded right to me. I was the talent, not an accountant. I made it, I spent it, but the truth was, I had no idea how much it all added up to. I just knew it was a lot and that my new Ferrari's license plate read "Sitch1" and the Bentley's was simply "Sitch." I had people to handle the rest of it. Businesspeople. People I trusted, like Marc.

That being said, ultimately, all of it was my responsibility. At the end of the day, I have no one to blame but myself for what would transpire. But back then, as a green, naïve rookie celebrity grappling with the excesses of new wealth and public adoration, the tax man was the farthest thing from my mind.

"Yeah?" I responded, not looking up from the phone.

Marc hesitated, then said, "Unless you just want to catch up with the IRS next year."

"Yeah, let's do that," I answered carelessly. "We'll get 'em next year."

Though I didn't realize it at the time, that single decision would plague me for years. My foolishness, years of intoxication, and lack of self-awareness would cost me so much. Yet also teach me so much. As with most things in life, with the bad comes some good.

I've had what seems like several lifetimes of both.

CHAPTER 1

MEET THE SITUATION

Linda Sorrentino (Mama Peaches), Mike's mother:

Mike and I both almost died during his birth. It's a miracle we even made it that far.

When I got pregnant with Mike in the fall of 1980, both his father and I were incredibly excited. We had two boys already, and we just knew this would finally be our little girl. But nothing with this pregnancy would go as planned.

Early on, I started to bleed and have pains, and my doctor informed me there was a good chance I would miscarry. I was devastated to think that I could lose this baby before it even had a chance at life. But as the months went on and I maintained strict bedrest, I became more optimistic that the pregnancy would go to full term.

It was already hot and sticky the morning of the Fourth of July in 1981 as my husband and I discussed our plans for the day; we would be attending a family barbeque celebrating Independence Day. I was eating breakfast when the phone rang, and as I stood to answer it, I felt fluid pouring out of me. I assumed my water had broken, but when I looked down, I saw a massive amount of blood on the kitchen floor. I was hemorrhaging.

When I got to the hospital, they placed me in a bed with my feet in the air and my head toward the ground in an attempt to stop the bleeding. Though I wasn't in labor, they told me they had to get the baby out and scheduled an emergency C-section.

When I woke from the general anesthesia, I was told that my baby was in intensive care and had been born blue for lack of oxygen. They said I had lost so much blood that a transfusion was needed. My placenta had partially ripped, and the doctors said that if it had fully torn away, both my son and I would have died. For the next several days, I was on very strong painkillers and unable to see my baby while we both recovered from the trauma.

I remember when it was finally time to leave the hospital and go home, a nurse came up to me. "What did you name your little boy?" she asked with a smile on her face.

"Michael Paul," I answered proudly. The change in her expression surprised me.

"Are you sure you want to name him that?" she said.

"Of course. Why?"

"Michaels are known for being very active and aggressive," she answered.

I scoffed. "Oh, that's not true," I said, pushing my bundle of joy toward the exit, ready to get home to my family.

For a while, the nurse's ominous comments carried no weight. Thankfully, Mike was a very good baby. My other two boys, Frank, six years old at the time, and Marc, two, were much more rambunctious at that age. As a baby and younger child, Mike was incredibly calm. I could place him in his playpen with a few toys, and he would sit for hours, playing silently. I actually asked his pediatrician if something was wrong with Mike because I wasn't used to such an easygoing boy. The doctor laughed and said that was just his personality. Calm and quiet. He told me to enjoy it, so I did.

Mike was such a sweet little boy. I remember when his cousin, a little girl six months older than him, would come over to play, she'd take his toys away. Most kids would get mad or grab them back, but Mike would just sit there and look at her, as if communicating, "Okay, go ahead. You can take those." He wouldn't cry or try to fight her.

That all changed sometime in middle school. My tranquil and shy boy became outgoing, assertive, and mischievous. He was always into something, though never anything too malicious. He was a prankster who was popular and extroverted with lots of friends. Our house was the neighborhood hangout with kids of all ages coming and going constantly. Usually, they were up to some shenanigans. Throughout

Mike's childhood, we received plenty of calls about his behavior from teachers and principals.

I remember once in high school, Mike was tired of waiting for the traffic jam leaving campus to clear, so he decided to jump the curb with his white Isuzu Rodeo and drive across the front lawn of the school. Unfortunately for him, the principal was standing right there and jumped in front of Mike's car, waving his arms for him to stop. That didn't hinder Mike, who abruptly swerved to avoid hitting the principal and kept going. I don't remember how we punished him for that one, but I'm sure it was severe. Mike was always grounded. His bedroom would often be stripped nearly empty, save for the bed, after we removed all his belongings as punishment. Those punishments never seemed to have much effect.

Even with all that, Mike was still a good kid. His escapades were never mean-spirited or ill-willed. He was just an energetic, carefree young man who would do anything and everything just as long as you told him not to.

Mike:

I grew up in a stereotypical Italian family, a shining example of the middle-class American dream. Food and family—those were the things most important in our home. Our Sorrentino (Dad's side) and Arena (Mom's) ancestors had emigrated from Italy to create wonderful lives for themselves and their families in America, allowing future generations to reap the benefits of their risks and hard work. I was a member of one such generation.

One side of my father's ancestors hailed from a town in the Naples region of Italy called Cavo di Terra in Santa Lucia. The other side came from Avellino. My great-grandfather immigrated to this country in 1906 at the age of fifteen with a total of sixteen dollars in his pocket. He spoke no English, received no government handouts, and knew only a few distant relatives in America. Yet he would raise eight children and become the proprietor of a thriving bakery on Henderson Avenue in

Staten Island that he ran until his death. Even before that, back in Italy, there are stories about Francesco Sorrentino marrying Carolina Pasquale. Carolina's father and brother were men of respect in their village and not people to be trifled with.

Both sides of my mother's family were Sicilian. Her father, Salvatore Arena, was one of sixteen children and grew up in the Little Italy section of New York City—Mulberry Street. Her mother—my grandmother—came from royal blood, the Barricas, including a baron with a castle and family crest in the old country. Once they all settled in America, they successfully ran various businesses and unions while following the American dream.

My parents worked hard and raised four happy, healthy kids, starting the family on Staten Island before eventually relocating to the suburbs of New Jersey. The oldest, my brother Frank, is followed by Marc, then me, with our little sister, Melissa, bringing up the rear.

We grew up very close, us four siblings. Marc and I are about two years apart, and we did everything together as kids. We shared a room, played sports together, and traveled the country for taekwondo competitions on a martial arts team our father coached. Marc was a black belt, I was a brown belt. A room in the basement grew full with our collected trophies.

I was a natural athlete, and sports always came easy. I excelled at football, though by the time I reached high school, I was more concerned with my looks, getting girls, and being popular than joining the team. I was one of the fastest players freshman year, the last year I played, but I never applied myself. I wish I had. I remember our father saying that I had the talent, but Marc had the work ethic and coachability; if we ever teamed up, we'd be unstoppable. Of course, years later, Uncle Sam would have his own opinion on the Sorrentino brothers dream team, but we'll get to that later.

Mom was a homemaker who never failed to have dinner on the table at five o'clock every evening. She always put out an amazing spread, whether it was manicotti, stuffed shells, chicken cutlets, fresh mashed potatoes, cavatelli and broccoli, spaghetti and meatballs, etc.

Sundays meant Sunday Sauce. Mama Peaches started her preparation early in the morning, her thick red sauce simmering throughout the day, filling the house with the smell of cooking tomatoes, meatballs, sausage, and braciole. To this day, Mama Peaches is still the best cook I've ever encountered. I've traveled the world and eaten at famous restaurants in Italy, and I'd put her cuisine up against any of those chefs'. I always say one day I'm going to open up a restaurant for my mom.

In my family, food made our house a home. It was an important value instilled early in my life and one that I teach to my son. We have as many meals together as possible. The Sorrentinos believe family is supposed to sit together and eat together. That's what's important in life—breaking bread and eating food made with love with the people you love.

My pops, Frank Sr., worked as an electrical engineer, and I can neither confirm nor deny whether he may or may not have had some, ahem, shall we say ties to a well-dramatized and maybe glamorized criminal organization known for its members wearing shiny suits and possessing last names generally ending in a vowel. That was pretty typical for an Italian neighborhood on Staten Island in the eighties.

The Mafia lifestyle was part of growing up in our community, and even when we moved out to Jersey, we saw its ripples. If anything, the Mafia was romanticized in my household. *Goodfellas* was always playing on the TV. Then, we would see those same types of guys whispering to each other at back tables in our neighborhood restaurants.

That's partially why we ended up leaving Staten Island—to get away from that life. My dad knew all the made guys from the neighborhood, and lots of the kids he had grown up with ended up in that line of work. I don't know to what extent he associated with them or if there was a specific incident that accelerated our departure from Staten Island, but the scent of the Mafia in our neighborhood was as ever-prevalent as freshly baking semolina bread and Aqua Velva aftershave.

I remember my dad bringing me to construction sites and introducing me to guys sitting around on lawn chairs playing cards while everyone else worked. I'd shake hands with so-and-so, clearly someone special. Well-respected. Then, on the way home, Dad would fill me in on who so-and-so was, who he was associated with, and why he was an important man.

My dad was a man's man, someone I always looked up to. A former Golden Gloves boxer. A tough guy. I heard countless stories about how no one would mess with him, how anytime a problem arose with his associates or his brothers, he would be the one called in to fix it. Pops was known for not hesitating to let his fists fly, and at every barbeque, my brothers and I would be regaled with stories about how our dad had never taken a beating. Pops looked, dressed, and sounded like Tony Soprano. Probably acted a little like him too.

When I was young, we lived in a white three-bedroom colonial with only one bathroom in the Sunset Hill section of Staten Island. Us kids attended P.S. 45 right down the street from our house. Then, when I turned six, we exited the city for greener pastures and a better life in New Jersey. We moved to Manalapan, an all-American city called just down the Garden State Parkway and over the Outerbridge Crossing from Staten Island.

While only thirty miles away, Manalapan was a totally different world from Staten Island and felt like a step up for us. Safe and clean with farms and open land everywhere, it was a great place to live and raise a family. That's where I attended elementary school, middle school, and high school, graduating from Manalapan High in 1999.

CHAPTER 2

MIS-EDUCATION

This may not come as much of a surprise, but I wasn't the most studious pupil. A solid C student. Poor academic results stemmed not from a lack of intelligence so much as a lack of effort. The quote, "I'm not here for a long time, I'm here for a good time," comes to mind. In high school, when I did attend class, I was more interested in being the center of attention than learning.

I was popular in school, albeit always in trouble. For as long as I can remember, I was the class clown and, like most class clowns, existed as the bane of my teachers' existence. My mother's phone number was usually posted on the chalkboard for everyone in class to see, a reminder to me that at a moment's notice, the teacher was willing and able to call her and report any infraction. I spent most of my class time passing notes, flirting with girls, and making smartass comments. Nothing vicious, but enough to encourage my teachers to keep a supply of Peptol handy in their desk drawers.

Hence why I previously referred to myself as the black sheep of the family. Marc got straight As, Frank was more of a mama's boy, and Melissa could do no wrong as the princess of the family. Then, there was me.

Once, during freshman year, my parents planned a rare but long overdue vacation for themselves. They were leery of leaving me and my brothers home alone, but knowing that Frank was the opposite of me (responsible), they decided to go and leave him in charge. I immediately convinced him and Marc to let me host a party with the promise that they would get a cut of the door—five dollars a head for a red Solo cup and access to kegs and a DJ.

Word got out to the neighboring towns, and soon, hundreds of young hormonal teenagers appeared from various local high schools. After hours of revelry, fights began to break out, their severity increasing until eventually the cops were called, and a full-on stampede broke out as people tried to escape. In the chaos of this mass exodus, someone got hit by a car, and months later, my parents would be targeted with a lawsuit from the injured kid's parents. It was definitely the party of the year and talked about throughout Monmouth County for some time, even if it did no favors for my reputation for mischief.

My aversion to authority took hold at a young age. You could pretty much guarantee Mike was going to do the opposite of whatever he was told to do. If you told me not to smoke weed, I was going to sell coke. If you told me to drive carefully, I would do donuts in the parking lot. In fact, right after I got my license, I smoked angel dust on the way to homecoming in Marc's hand-me-down Pontiac Sunfire that our father gave me…and wrecked it after hitting a sewer grate and bottoming out. As the car steamed and smoked, I sprinted from the scene. After I called my father, he rushed to the scene and told the police he had been the one driving when the power steering failed. Thanks for taking one for the team, Pops.

I always pushed the envelope, resulting in a never-ending torrent of punishments and reprimands from parents, teachers, and, on occasion, police. At home, that meant doors being detached from their hinges, my computer and TV being taken away, and months-long groundings. A never-ending chore list was another popular parental punishment. After school, I was forced to come home and do everything from mowing the lawn to mopping the floors, depending on most recent transgressions. Outside of the home, the ramifications were a little more severe.

My first time ever having a sip of alcohol just so happened to coincide with my first arrest. That alone should have been a sign that I was incapable of enjoying substances the same way as others. Unfortunately, it would be many years and a series of serious struggles before I could make that connection and initiate change. As a rambunctious teenager, I just wanted to be one of the fellas and drink beer after some older guys I hung out with secured a keg. They relocated it to Hawkins Park for consumption, and when I heard about the impromptu party, I waited until midnight before sneaking out to join.

Shortly after I arrived, as my palms tightly gripped the keg's cold edges, my feet straight up in the air and secured firmly by Johnny D (who I'm still good friends with to this day), a bright light interrupted my first-ever keg stand.

What the hell is that? My adolescent brain thought as I choked on beer. A chilling voice of authority reached my ears: "Put the young man down." Johnny D unceremoniously dropped my legs.

Next thing I knew, I was in cuffs. Arrested after my first sip of booze. Damn. My father was the one who had to come pick my sorry ass up at the police station, and man, was he angry. Not so much because I was drinking but because I got caught. I can still hear him screaming obscenities at me.

Both my brothers came in the car with him for some reason, probably eager to witness yet another spectacle of their little brother getting in trouble since they never did. I crawled in the back behind Frank, who was perched excitedly in the front passenger seat. His responsibility during the drive home was to hold the wheel and steer as our father occasionally reached into the back seat and tried to strangle me with both hands à la Homer Simpson. Hey, it was the nineties. That stuff flew back then. I could only laugh and squirm in his grip.

I learned very little from that experience. Let's just say that getting arrested left me undeterred. I was never a big drinker but did enjoy crossing boundaries. However, after so many times brushing up against the authorities and getting my hand slapped, I started trying to be more smooth about it, concocting plots that distanced myself from the deed.

Case in point, our senior class prank: In an organized and coordinated attack, an unidentified conglomerate of assailants simultaneously released mice in the school cafeteria one afternoon during the last month of school. It was such a shocking and brazen operation that only a true future prank war champion could have masterminded the operation. Despite my best effort to insulate myself from any ties to said prank, including assigning other classmates to purchase the offending rodents from a local pet store and going so far as to stay home sick the day of the event, my mom still received a call from the vice principal,

Mr. Grandy, placing blame squarely on me for requiring the fire department to shut down the school in a ramification covered extensively by the local newspaper.

When all was said and done, the administration concluded I had orchestrated the entire thing. Allegedly, of course. They accused Michael Sorrentino of being the kingpin, the mastermind behind a conspiracy so devious, so underhanded, that only The Situation could have pulled it off—and as a result, I was suspended from our senior prom.

I have no doubt the Manalapan High School staff breathed a sigh of relief when it came time for Michael Sorrentino to matriculate, which I barely managed to do. Even though The Situation hadn't yet been invented, I still managed to turn the graduation ceremony into one.

Graduation day, 1999. Manalapan High's next batch of future leaders, bright-eyed and bushy-tailed, brimmed with enthusiasm as they lined up in cap and gown. A stage had been erected on the football field, the stands and folding chairs filled with friends, family, and advancing seniors. Each took their turn walking across the dais, receiving their share of smattering applause and collecting a stiff piece of paper designating them a high school graduate.

"Michael Sorrentino," announced Ms. Grey, the principal, as I sauntered onto the stage to collect my diploma. You know I looked dapper in the school's red graduation regalia, tanned, with a fresh haircut and just the right amount of gel applied. I was definitely feeling myself when I offered a little wink to my cheering section in the stands as I approached Ms. Grey at the podium.

Suddenly, I threw my body forward, completing what I can only assume was a perfect cartwheel across the stage. However, in my exuberance and desire to entertain, or maybe because of the adrenaline that came from being allowed to actually leave high school a graduate, I misjudged the principal's proximity, overshot the landing, and accidentally kicked Ms. Grey right in the face. After tossing out a sputtering apology through nervous laughter, I was sent on my way empty-handed. Needless to say, the administration was not amused, and instead of me leaving graduation with that diploma, it was withheld and eventually mailed to me.

Those were the types of pranks I propagated and excelled at during my school years. Again, nothing malevolent. I wasn't a bully. I didn't hurt anyone. All things considered, I managed to make it through high school relatively unscathed. I made it, at least. Walking a razor's edge but with no real damage done.

But in case it's not already clear, I was the type of kid that if you told me not to do something, not only would I do it twice, I would take pictures.

Kind of like a reality star.

CHAPTER 3
MALE STRIPPING

I had no idea what I wanted to do with my life after graduation. No particular career had piqued my interest as of yet. I gave college a shot because that's what you're supposed to do next, but that didn't last long.

I did have a desire to break into show business, and everywhere I went, people told me, "Man, you gotta do something with that body." I mean, I did have what would become the most recognizable eight-pack in history. Even before the *Jersey Shore* days, people were in disbelief when I lifted my shirt up. They couldn't believe my abs were real. After displaying a mind-blown face, they would invariably ask if they were implants or airbrushed. The answer: Neither. They're real, and they're spectacular (that's for all you fellow *Seinfeld* fans), partly due to great genetics but also because of my focus on self-care. I worked out twice a day, maintained a strict diet, and stayed hydrated. But yeah, mostly due to genetics.

Back then, my life revolved around looking and feeling my best. I just needed to figure out how to make my abs work for me, aside from attracting the opposite sex. At that point, I still didn't truly comprehend the value of what God had gifted me. But I was learning.

Before there ever was a Situation, there was Mikey Abs. That's what they called me in high school and college. In fact, when my boys wanted to meet girls at the club, they would call me over. "Mike, show 'em," they'd say. I'd laugh, lift up my shirt, and everybody would go nuts. Girls wanted to touch them, take pictures with them. Guys couldn't believe what they were seeing. They were just amazed to be next to such a specimen.

How could I turn that into a paying job?

I was aware of the male revue show at Club Abyss in South Amboy and had always kinda thought, *yeah, I could do that.* And why not?

During that period of my life, my motivation for almost everything I did revolved around getting girls. You're telling me I could get paid to have them grope me? What could be better? I was young, in great shape, and stripping was a way to flaunt my God-given gift: my body. A win-win situation.

So I did it. I must have been nineteen or twenty when I started stripping. I know it was right about the time I was introduced to painkillers because I remember asking the other guys if they had a Percocet or Vicodin before going on stage. They looked at me like I was crazy. "Nah, what's that?" I was like, *these guys are missing out.* They had alcohol, coke, ecstasy, and even GHB, but painkillers were pretty rare back then.

Stripping was strictly a weekend job that lasted only a few months. Honestly, I liked it. At the time, I was working at a gym and waiting tables at the Main Street Bistro in Freehold (where I got fired two or three times). I was sick of manual labor. I was all about working smarter, not harder. Male revue was easy and fun. I'd show up, walk around with no shirt on (well, maybe a little less than that...), and get paid well. I served drinks in my Calvin Kleins and offered lap dances and massages: twenty bucks for a lap dance, ten for a massage, if you're keeping score at home.

The whole thing was pretty nuts. Imagine punching in for your shift at work and having one of your customers ask what it costs to perform oral sex on you. Good question—what does one charge for that? I actually had to contemplate an answer. I was like, "Wow, you want to pay me to do that?" (I can neither confirm nor deny whether I ever took any patrons up on the offer. A gentleman never tells.)

Those escapades happened almost nightly at Club Abyss. To a young, single man, it was an ideal situation, at least at first. But soon, I became jaded and started to think differently about the opposite sex. Mentally, I put myself in the position of the groom who was at home thinking his fiancée was out for ladies' night, and meanwhile, there's a DIHM. Oh my God, can you imagine? This moral dilemma was one of the reasons why I hung up my stripper boots.

Another reason presented itself after what would be my last night headlining at the male revue. Patrons' birthdays were a big deal at the club. Whenever a woman in the audience was celebrating her birthday, they'd bring her up front and set out a chair for her under the spotlight. All eyes on the birthday girl. The DJ would queue up the Jodeci or Blackstreet while her girlfriends shrieked and cheered her on, estrogen and alcohol mixing to form pheromonal intoxication. Then, I'd sashay out on stage, all oiled up, wearing only a red, white, and blue thong (since I was born on the Fourth of July) and a grin. I'd climb on, over, and under the lucky lady, straddling her, rubbing on her, giving her the lap dance of her life. At the end of the day, it was hard work, but someone had to do it. I felt like this all-American boy was performing a vital service, letting these women act out their fantasies.

This particular night, after several such birthday dances, I got home late to find my mom and dad waiting for me at the front door. That wasn't too uncommon, walking into an ambush and getting accosted for something I'd done wrong, but this time, I could see their roles were reversed. While my dad was in the background stifling a smile, my mom was about as angry as I'd ever seen her. The setup made me curious. What had they caught on to now? Then, as soon as I crossed the threshold, probably still smelling like baby oil, an umbrella clutched in my mother's grip began to rain blows upon my head.

"Ma! What are you doing? What's wrong?" I called out, trying to protect myself.

"Where! Were! You?" she sputtered between blows.

"I was at work, catching a late shift at the restaurant!" I lied. That was my go-to excuse when I was stripping.

"No! You! Weren't! My girlfriend called me! It was her birthday, and she told me that my son Michael gave her a lap dance at some male strip club!"

Oh, damn. Busted. I knew I'd recognized that lady... Nothing I could do but eat the umbrella while my dad continued trying to keep a straight face. I managed to swallow my own laughter for the most part. That's the way it is in the Italian culture. A little corporal punishment with whatever object is handy. An umbrella, the wooden spatula, two hands shaking with anger. No big deal. You mess up, you earn a light beating from your parents. I know what some readers are going say, but it's all good. It comes with the territory. Though I have to admit, as a result of those punishments during my adolescence, I now suffer from a rare psychological condition known as "having respect for others."

CHAPTER 4

THE LOVE OF MY LIFE

After my mother's inadvertent discovery of my new career, morals (and embarrassment) took over. Shortly thereafter, I quit stripping for good. The juice just wasn't worth the squeeze—girls already threw themselves at me at the club, and besides, my next entrepreneurial foray meant I wouldn't need the money.

In the meantime, I grew stagnant. I didn't have any plans, didn't know what to do with myself. I still had big aspirations and dreams but wasn't yet sure how to execute them. I had no real marketable skills—or at least I hadn't yet figured out how to properly market them outside of taking my clothes off. I was content to simply continue enjoying being a kid. Partying. Hanging with my boys. And I felt like that was okay. Time was on my side. I had no doubt that whatever I ended up doing, it would be huge.

Turns out, I was right again, even if no one else believed me at the time. Looking back now, I can say that perhaps my biggest flex is that I accomplished everything I said I was going to. But if you knew me during the years leading up to *Jersey Shore*, I wouldn't have blamed you for not believing my bravado.

After a couple years of drifting, I decided to give college another shot. Not because I was focused on education but because I thought it would be a good placeholder while I continued trying to figure out what to do with my life. When I re-enrolled at Brookdale Community College for my second go-around at the school, I was essentially kicking the can down the road. I'd previously attended—er, signed up for classes at—Brookdale after high school, before transferring to Kean College in Union, New Jersey, and ultimately failing out.

Going back to Brookdale ended up being the best decision of my life.

Not because of the education I received there—Brookdale is a fine school, I'm sure, but I can't claim to utilize many of the lessons learned earning my associate degree in business management. However, my second enrollment did lead to me meeting the person who has had the single biggest impact on my life, bar none. It's where I made the acquaintance of one Lauren Elizabeth Pesce, my future wife, best friend, mother of my children, and better half. A woman who went on to fight for me when I wouldn't fight for myself. Someone who showed me the meaning of living your best life, who ignited a flame in me to be a better man and inspired me to fight some of life's toughest battles with integrity, honor, and faith. Who gave me my beautiful children, a wonderful home, and the tough love and structure we would need to survive and overcome the many trials that awaited. Although small in stature, this strong-spirited Italian girl would be the one to tame The Situation and turn this boy into an honorable man. To this day, I love her with all my heart.

But on the first day of math class back in 2004, she represented nothing more than a cute girl grabbing my attention from across the classroom. You know how it is when you get your school schedule: A little fluctuation in the sternum. Excitement to see who's in your classes. Maybe some friends you know, maybe a cute girl... In this case, a few of the former and exactly one of the latter.

I remember walking into the classroom and scanning for familiar faces and a strategic seat placement. I was sporting a fresh haircut, rocking my gray and orange Puma jumpsuit, carrying the matching hat in hand rather than on my head because no way was I going to risk messing up my hair wearing it. The hat was an insurance policy—if throughout the wear and tear of the day, my hair got out of place and wasn't perfect, the hat would be waiting in the wings to keep my look intact.

I hadn't created the GTL moniker yet, but it had already been my daily routine for years. My schedule consisted of going to the gym, then tanning, and finally, ensuring I rocked an awesome outfit for the day— the foundation of what Pauly and I would christen as "GTL" in season one of *Jersey Shore*.

Even in college, my day always revolved around fitness—going to the gym, eating healthy meals, and hydrating accordingly to ensure I looked and felt my best. I've always taken pride in my appearance and practiced self-care and self-love religiously ever since I can remember. There was no doubt I was showing up to the first day of school fresh to death. I've always said confidence is the best accessory to any outfit, and I'd never lacked confidence.

A sense of optimism and newness permeated the environment as I took in my surroundings. Possibilities abounded. The world was my oyster. I remember selecting a seat at the back of the classroom where I could soak in the whole scene. I immediately took notice of this absolutely beautiful girl sitting up front. She was tiny and blond, which wasn't my normal type, but I was drawn to this minute package of cuteness. I always went for brunettes; this was the first time in memory I had been super attracted to a blond, at least enough to entertain seriously dating one. Yes, with that first sighting, I could already see myself being exclusive with this girl, and I didn't yet know who she was.

Next class, I made sure to take an open seat at the front, right next to her, and hit her with that ol' Sorrentino charm. Some other dude was feeling this girl too, trying the same game. He sat on the other side of her and was definitely hitting on her, feeling out the situation to see if he could get her number. Honestly, I wasn't too worried about him. I had confidence in my game. It's like one of my lines in *Jersey Shore*: "Listen, if I was in the club and you walked in with your girl, if I was you, I'd be worried. I'd grab my girl real quick if I saw me in the room." So yeah, I wasn't sweating this dude.

For the next few classes, we all sat together. We were a trio. It was a game, and you know there are rules. You can't go too hard and you can't go too soft.

I thought to myself, *I'm gonna sit back and let him, you know, do what he needs to do. Then, I'm gonna come in when it's my turn to talk, and I'm going to sweep this girl off her feet.*

And that's just what I did. I let him do his thing, and I did mine. Let the best man win. At the end of the day, I got her number. I got the date.

Lauren Sorrentino, Mike's wife:

When I first met Mike in class, I found him very charismatic and charming. I could also tell he was a little bit mischievous, which I liked. It was pretty obvious he wasn't exactly married to the idea of school and was instead just going through the motions. I could empathize—I was doing the same thing. I was still super young and had just moved back home to Jersey after leaving a college in Florida that I didn't like. Like Mike, I was trying to figure out what I wanted to do with my life. We immediately connected on not just our uncertain futures but our shared Italian heritage. He was cute, clean-cut, fit, and put together, and when Mike asked me for my number, I readily gave it to him.

Once Mike and I started dating, it didn't take long for us to get close. He was such a fun, nice guy. I loved being around him. People always ask me if he was cocky, but he wasn't at all. That's simply a persona he leaned into when he had the opportunity to make a living off it. But I never saw that. He never exuded that quality to me. Cocky is the last word I would use to describe Mike.

Even before he was on TV, Mike was a local celebrity. He was like the mayor of Monmouth County and the shore, and he was only in his early twenties. Whenever we went out, whether it was to dinner or shopping at the mall, Mike knew everyone, and everyone knew him. And he talked to *everyone*, anywhere we went. It didn't matter if it was the McDonald's drive-through or a club in the city. Everybody loved him. They treated him great. That's how he's always been. Popular. A people person and big talker.

Even now, when he's recognized everywhere he goes, he loves it. Anyone who approaches him gets the time of day from Mike. He appreciates his fans and treats them with the utmost kindness and respect. To this day, I don't think he's ever not taken a photo with a fan who asked.

CHAPTER 5
DRUG DEALING

Laurens and I became inseparable as soon as we started dating. When I found out her last name was Pesce, I was like, "Damn!" I'd always been such a big fan of Joe Pesce in *Goodfellas* and *Casino*. It was a neat factor that brought out my inner child. Like we were meant to be.

As we got to know each other better, I found out she was old-school Italian like me with the same family values. Her father was a farmer who owned a landscaping company and had done very well for himself. They lived in a really nice, wealthy town called Holmdel, New Jersey, and I remember as I'd drive past all those huge, beautiful houses to pick her up, I'd think, *Someday, I'd like to live in one of these homes. To settle down and raise a family here.* Which is pretty funny because Lauren and I now own one of those beautiful houses in Holmdel, about five minutes from where she was raised.

Because of Lauren, I'm currently living my dream. I love our story. It's a great lesson about never giving up on true love; it feels like the stars aligned for us. We both have a lot of appreciation for the wonderful life we have and pride in how we've battled through and overcome each adversity along the way.

But there was a long way to go before The Situation would settle down and live a peaceful life in the 'burbs with the white picket fence. I mentioned earlier embarking on a new career after early retirement from the stripping life. I had fallen into drug dealing.

When I was nineteen, my parents went through a divorce, and I had to maintain a certain lifestyle expectation that I could no longer rely on them for. Selling weed to my buddies seemed almost too easy not to do. But like everything in my life, I took it to the extreme, and soon, I was moving pounds of weed and ounces of cocaine every week.

I'm not claiming to have been some kingpin, but like I said, similar to most Italian kids growing up in that environment, I'd always looked up to Mafia figures. The outlaws. Mobsters. By no stretch of the imagination was I a mobster, but some of my activities mirrored those of that type of person. I was a hustler to be sure. All my boys aspired to be like that, and I fell in love with the lifestyle.

I began making weekly runs to Brooklyn, where I'd pick up, say, thirty pounds of weed and ten ounces of coke. On the arm, they called it, or on consignment. I'd take it back to Jersey, where I developed a little crew to help me move the product. We'd sell out pretty quickly, then pay back the $75,000 or so I owed on the next week's trip to Brooklyn. Rinse and repeat.

The money was spectacular. I spent it as fast as it came in. I lived at my dad's house, so there weren't many expenses. The drug proceeds mostly went to nice clothes and shoes, a state-of-the-art flat screen and entertainment center for my bedroom, a BMW 5 Series, and keeping the safe stacked with cash.

Then, there was the partying. After receiving our weekly product shipment from the connect and completing our drop-offs without hiccups or police interference, me and the crew would go out to celebrate. I did those nights the same way I did everything—extra and over the top. We'd usually start at Red Lobster for a gargantuan dinner, then hit up the strip club and make it rain before heading to a lounge for VIP bottle service. After that, we'd usually post up in a hotel suite to celebrate further with strippers or other girls we'd met at the club. I took care of the squad, paying for everything. Thousands of dollars a night, which was cool with me. Easy come, easy go.

I was a good drug dealer. Organized, punctual, and honest. All qualities rare but appreciated in that industry. Most of my friends worked for me, and it felt like I was the boss of my own little organization. I'd give some of the guys I trusted weed and coke on consignment, and they'd pay me back before my own payment was due. We dealt wholesale amounts, and often, I wouldn't even touch the drugs. I designed a system where a friend, often my neighbor and best friend, Chris, whom I trusted even though he was a loose cannon, would pick up thirty pounds or so for me. The weight would be earmarked for other dealers, and he'd drop off six pounds here, ten pounds there. If we did touch it, it was only for a couple of hours. Then, it was out of our hands.

There was another tactic we utilized when transporting a lot of weight. We'd send one car in front of the person transporting the drugs and have a clean car follow him. That way, if he got pulled over, one of us could swerve and drive recklessly so the cop would follow the other car. Luckily, we never had to employ that tactic, but that's not to say I didn't have my share of run-ins with the law.

One time, as I sped along Route 9, not far from where I now live, stupidly smoking weed in my black-on-black Bimmer, the old red and blues popped up in the rearview. Shit—I was getting pulled over! I cracked the windows and tried to air the car out but to no avail. I went through a mental checklist about what was in the car. Thank God, I had finished my drop-offs already and didn't have any weight on me. All the cops found was an eighth of weed and a bowl, and I ended up getting arrested for possession. I'm lucky that I only had personal usage on me instead of the pounds that were often in my trunk, or it could have been really bad. Sometimes, it's better to be lucky than good. Especially when you're being dumb.

Times were good. I was making great money while ensuring my crew got paid. Nobody got robbed. Everybody paid on time. I had a nice, well-oiled machine and became one of the biggest distributors in Monmouth County. If things were dry, it was because we ran out.

But as we know, that life is not sustainable. I was already a pretty well-known guy in that part of Jersey, and being the weed and coke guy only elevated my notoriety. It was only a matter of time before it all came crashing down.

At some point, my brother Marc got a call from a cop he knew. The cop told him I was on a list of known drug dealers, and there was a task force targeting me. When I learned that, I decided to cool it for a little. But I always went back to drug dealing. I was drawn to the fast, lucrative lifestyle. The stakes were high, and the rewards matched the risk. I related it to being a businessman, an entrepreneur. I kept running back to it, even though I knew it was only a matter of time before someone robbed me or ratted on me. It was a game of cat and mouse, and I kept rolling the dice despite the odds being stacked against me.

Like they say in *Goodfellas*, "As far back as I can remember, I always wanted to be a gangster." Now, I thought I was one.

Lauren:

I knew what he was doing. I mean, I didn't know the extent of it—I was super naïve—but back then, it was mainly weed, which didn't seem too concerning to me. I'd lived in a sheltered environment where all I'd ever seen in my life was weed, and back then it didn't seem like a big thing to me.

But I didn't like it. I'm not someone who ever enjoyed drinking or doing drugs. I'm different from Mike in that I don't have an addictive personality in the least. I've definitely tried things, but the negatives—feeling sick or hungover—always kept me from wanting to do them again. Mike, of course, has the exact opposite personality.

We were always together, so of course I saw a ton of suspicious activity. I'd go with him on collections sometimes and saw all the cash. I knew it was his main source of income, and he seemed to have a lot of money.

His whole life, his family had basically given him everything, and when I met him, his parents were going through a messy divorce. All their kids were in adulthood, and their parents were like, you know, "figure your life out." Not that that's an excuse, but he didn't have a career path or certain life skills to fall back on. And I think there was a certain lifestyle and status he wanted to maintain; this was how he could do it.

That type of thing wasn't rare where we grew up. It was the culture in the area and probably why I wasn't really scared about what he was doing. Organized crime was glorified, so a kid selling weed didn't set off any alarms in my mind. Things always happened where people were like, "Oh, I got a deal on this, wink wink," or joked about "Don't ask where it came from—it fell off the back of a truck." That was just Jersey.

Mike:

Lauren didn't love what I was doing, but we were so young, we didn't really see the danger. At that age, you don't have many cares in the world. If we were fearless, it was because we didn't know any better due to a lack of life experience. Besides, we had a bit of a Bonnie and Clyde fantasy going.

Sometimes, Lauren would come along with me on collections. When we got home, she'd count stacks of cash, then line them up in my safe. Sometimes, I'd have to placate her by saying I was going to stop soon and go legit. For the most part, I meant it. Especially when I felt the heat around the corner. I knew this lifestyle was fleeting and had a shelf life; I didn't plan on it ending badly. Then again, no one does. I mean, no one wants to go to prison. Of course, if you want to make God laugh, tell him about your plans.

Despite the risks, Laurens and I were happy. I continued conducting my business and living a lavish lifestyle, taking my crew out to the club and popping bottles or Lauren to dine at an expensive restaurant where we ordered anything we wanted. Money was no object. I bought her clothes and bags and jewelry and shoes and things, which was kind of over the top for two young kids in community college. Not like I can now, but for a couple in our early twenties, we were doing alright.

Our love for each other flourished over those next few years. I respected how strong and fiery she was. Lauren had her own point of view and her own voice and wasn't afraid to make herself heard. We moved in together, making our home in a cute little one-bedroom apartment in Old Bridge, New Jersey. Things were good between us—for a while.

But then, I began an affair. One that would last years and eventually tear us apart. One that would have such a deep, dark impact on my life and on those I loved that its effects are still felt to this day. Like most trysts, it started innocently at first. Flirting. I'd been dabbling for years with few repercussions. But the relationship had grown. It went from hanging out every once in a while to every day. I became dependent on it. Without realizing it, I found I could no longer live without it.

My love affair was with the devil: prescription opiates.

CHAPTER 6

A RELATIONSHIP WITH THE DEVIL

I've never really enjoyed uppers. Even though I dealt coke and experimented regularly in my twenties, I never liked how it made me feel. Of course, apropos to my personality, I couldn't do just a single line or a couple key bumps in the bathroom stall at the club like my boys did. Because I overdid everything, I often drank so much that doing coke was the only way to keep the party going. If not, I'd pass out drunk. And once I started doing it, I had to do *all* the coke. Like to the point where I would get so high the paranoia was uncontrollable. It was almost comical how often I ended up barricading myself in a bathroom or hotel room because I believed the FBI or DEA was coming to get me. Skin crawling, I'd see and hear things that weren't there, sweating profusely as my heart pounded out of my chest. I hated the feeling so much I'd desperately seek a downer like Xanax to stave off the comedown. Anything to make me not feel that way.

Since I was already experimenting with prescription pills, when the introduction with the devil was made, I willingly reached out and shook his hand. Here's how that connection first occurred:

Many of the different neighborhoods in Manalapan connect to each other, making it easy to navigate from one development to another. It was common to bunk into people who lived in adjacent neighborhoods and influence each other with whatever mischief we had going on. My crew and I were always hustling, turning and burning, and making deals where we found them, often right around our parents' homes where most of us still lived.

Someone has a connect in Freehold Borough for fish scale cocaine? What's the number? We'll flip a few ounces. Some dude at a party can get elbows (that's what we called pounds of weed) *of Purple Haze at a good price?*

We'll take fifty, chop it, and get rid of it locally. That's just how we wheeled and dealed.

One day, when I was nineteen, Chris, my best friend I mentioned who lived across the street, told me about a kid in an adjoining neighborhood whose grandmother had cancer and a steady supply of Percocet. He asked me if I'd ever tried it before.

I'd been prescribed some lower-level painkillers for a previous hernia surgery as well as by the dentist after getting my wisdom teeth out, so I guess you could say I already had a little bit of a taste for them. But no real experience yet.

Chris had secured ten-milligram Percocet pills, which we called bananas. I remember we were driving in his car and we each put one in our mouth. I believe we sucked on them, letting the bitterness dissolve on our tongues. The taste was terrible. But soon, an amazing feeling came over me. I felt no pain. I remember thinking, *Wow, I've never felt like this before. Imagine feeling like this all the time…* We looked at each other in disbelief.

"Wow, do you feel that?" Chris asked.

"Yeah. I can't believe one pill can make you feel this good," I answered, astounded. It was as if we had just been introduced to a whole new world. Something new and beautiful and amazing. The world of opiates.

I loved it. I wanted more, again, always. I had no knowledge about the dangers of prescription pills. Addiction and dependency were not things I was aware of or worried about. If anything, these seemed safer than the other drugs I was selling and doing. These at least came from a doctor. How could they hurt? But most importantly, they made me feel great. All that wasted time on cocaine. I discovered opiates were my true love.

This was before I met Lauren. Back when I'd only been selling drugs for a short period of time. In the beginning of my love affair, I only took painkillers when I could get them, which wasn't that often. They were hard to come by back then. Like little nuggets of gold. You had to know someone. You had to hustle. Fortunately—or unfortunately—for me, I knew everyone and was always on the hustle.

Then opiates started to become more prevalent. More accessible. I'd hear about someone getting a script for one hundred bananas. Boom, I'd buy half of them. Someone else had strawberries, seven-point-five-milligram Percocet. I'd buy them all, selling half and squirreling away the other half for personal use. Then there were the benzos—Xanax, Valium, and Klonopin. I loved those too and stocked up whenever I could get them.

Still, I was only dabbling. I'd get whatever pills I could whenever I could, holding them like my own personal treasure. Sometimes, I'd come home after collections, throw on a movie, and pop a Perc or a Xany bar from own private stash, maybe have a girl over. Just chill. I had not a care in the world. No bills, money hand over fist, with more girls than I could juggle. I was a neighborhood celebrity. Life was good.

As time went on, the frequency of availability increased, and so too did my usage. My tolerance grew, and I began needing to take more and more just to get the same feeling. Still, I was able to keep it under control, popping pills casually for several years. Then, right after meeting Lauren, the opiate game escalated. The affair grew stronger right under my new girlfriend's nose.

One day, a kid in our class offered us each a Roxicet. I didn't even know what a Roxicet was, but when he removed a tiny blue pill from this little sleeve attached to his keychain, I remember thinking, *How strong can this be?* I mean, the pill was a fraction of the size of the Percocet and Vicodin I was used to taking. I figured it wouldn't do much to someone as experienced as I was. Lauren and I each tried one without having any idea of what it would do to us.

Wow. Just…wow. It made me feel great. I loved everything about it. I'd developed some type of tolerance from experimenting with opiates for a few years but had never felt anything like this. I couldn't believe this tiny little pill was overpowering me. (I later discovered one Roxicet was the same strength as three Percocets.) It felt amazing.

On the other hand, Lauren, who had no experience with painkillers, had a different reaction. She hated it. She couldn't even walk. I remember being like, "Come on, Drama Queen. What do you mean you can't walk or see?" But she was floored by that little pill. Yeah, at five foot and ninety-five pounds with no tolerance, I guess that made sense. She couldn't stand the feeling and never did them again.

As for me? Like Lauren said, we are opposites. I immediately went back to the kid and tried to get more. Then more.

Sourcing those designer, heavy-duty prescription pain pills became a full-time job. I don't think I was fully hooked at this point, but it certainly was an itch I needed to scratch. My curiosity about the existence of such a powerful pill and how I could get my hands on more consumed me.

I still moved the weed and coke, but the now-torrid love affair with opiates became my priority. Most of my focus shifted to that endeavor. I wasn't the only one in America cheating on my life with this chemical relationship. This was the early 2000s. An epidemic was expanding on a tidal wave of corrupt doctors and a greedy pharmaceutical industry. Synthetic opiates were now everywhere. Legit doctors were being trained to not allow their patients to experience any amount of pain and would readily prescribe these new wonder drugs for minor complaints. It was common knowledge that if you went to a doctor and said you felt back or neck pain, you could usually get a script for painkillers.

Worse, a proliferation of non-legit doctors exploded upon the scene. Oh, they had medical degrees and prescription pads (especially the latter) but no interest in practicing real medicine. Pill mills had become too profitable, way easier than seeing real patients and diagnosing real illnesses. For two hundred bucks cash, these doctors could write a prescription in minutes and see fifty "patients" a day. That's where the money was at. Those were the doctors my squad and I sought.

We were always on the hunt for lenient doctors. Those we could either fool with fake injuries or who would take cash to write a script. We'd pass these doctor referrals around as treasured intel. I made appointments with doctors in all the neighboring towns, complaining mostly about back pain. If most people get an MRI on their back, chances are something's going to show up on it. With my years of lifting and general wear and tear, I could easily make the case for Oxys or at least Percocet over a herniated disc on an MRI. I think I even tried to convince myself—and eventually Lauren—that I suffered from an actual ailment, but that was bullshit. I had no pain. I was just good at feigning injury to get drugs.

Eventually, I procured a doctor in Marlboro who proved to be the equivalent of hitting an opioid jackpot. This lady started dishing out scripts to me whenever I wanted them for like 180 Roxicets, 120 Oxys, and Xanax to go to sleep. We considered the discovery of that doctor to be the greatest find of all time. Of course, having an unending supply of highly addictive narcotics is not a good thing long term, but for me at the time, it was the opiate dream. I never had to worry about running out of pills. At least not for a while.

In all my years of experimenting with prescription drugs, this was the first time I had a ready, steady, reliable supply of anything I wanted. No hustling necessary, no constant attempts to doctor shop, just one predictable supply of the devil's pellets. I thought it was what I wanted, and at the time, it was. But my habit began to impact my life. Without realizing it, I was fully and totally dependent. This was the beginning of an end that would take years to reach.

By this point, Lauren and I had been together for three or four years and were living together as a happy couple in Old Bridge. But a lot of that was on the surface. When one party is more focused on their relationship with drugs than on their relationship with their significant other, it puts a major strain on the couple.

As I said, I tried to convince her the pills I constantly popped were for legitimate pain, and for a while, she bought it. Why wouldn't she? After all, they were prescribed by my doctor. We still didn't understand the dangers of abusing prescription drugs. Lauren was an innocent girl from the suburbs of New Jersey. How could she have known her boyfriend was turning into a drug addict in front of her eyes? She couldn't have, even if she did recognize that *something* was wrong. As did I, even if I refused to acknowledge it at the time.

Our relationship suffered. I lost my sex drive, and we were no longer intimate. I didn't work, barely had the energy to hustle, and spent any drug profits I had left on pills. It got to where I could no longer pay the bills. I let the rent get three months behind. We were being threatened with eviction. I began to take bigger risks, selling prescriptions. The more I had, the more I took. When you're hooked, there's never enough. It's a vicious, illogical cycle I found myself wrapped in. I consumed more and more, which made my supply more likely to run out. When that happened, I would experience severe withdrawals. As I approached my mid-twenties and the claws of dependency and addiction dug themselves deeper into me, I was concerned with only one thing: finding pills and getting high. Or, more accurately, not getting sick. And it was killing the best relationship I'd ever had.

One day, Chris came to me and said he knew someone who worked at a hospital. This guy wasn't stealing pills or even individual scripts. He was stealing whole boxes of blank prescription pads—thousands of individual notes—from one of the doctors. That meant an absolute unlimited supply of painkillers. We just had to figure out how to write our own prescriptions, then find the pharmacies to fill them. All we needed were the balls to see if this cockamamie scheme would work.

We started where all enterprising young men go when they need information, legal or otherwise: Google. After an evening of research, we knew exactly what information was needed on a prescription and what the doctor lingo meant. We learned that "QID" meant four times a day and "TID" was three times a day. The frequency had to coincide with the number. For example, if we were prescribing ourselves thirty-milligram Oxys to take three times a day for a month, we'd make it out for ninety pills, using the required shorthand. Four times a day, 120. Luckily, all doctors have horrible handwriting, and since we'd been filling scripts for years, we knew how to scribble the signature so the pharmacy wouldn't know the difference.

It actually worked. I remember the first time we filled a forged script. When the pharmacist handed me that crinkled wax bag with a bottle holding ninety Oxys, Chris and I shared a wide-eyed look of disbelief. What Pandora's Box had we just opened?

For months, we filled prescriptions at pharmacies all across New Jersey and the New York metro area. Hundreds of them. Sometimes, we'd sell the pills; sometimes, we'd sell filled-out scripts. We consumed hundreds, if not thousands, of pills. Every day, all day. I officially had access to an unlimited supply of Percocet, Vicodin, oxycodone, and Roxicet, not to mention Xanax, Valium, and Klonopin. It had all begun by taking a pill here or there just to feel good and experiment, but eventually, the dream turned into a nightmare. I now needed this substance just to not feel violently ill. That realization was eye-opening because I was the one responsible for subjecting myself to a sickness I had never known existed. I had recklessly and foolishly kicked in a locked door to hell and walked right through.

It was a normal Saturday afternoon. The sun was shining, a glorious fall day. My cousin and I hit up a pharmacy five minutes down the road from me and Lauren's house on Route 18 in East Brunswick. We'd used it before but not too many times, so we figured it was above suspicion. I handed my forged script to the pharmacist, then left to get a slice at the pizza joint next door, kind of like setting an alibi. My cousin waited for his prescription of 180 oxycodone thirty-milligram pills to be filled. Nothing out of the ordinary for us.

Suddenly, the parking lot filled with cops, lights and sirens blaring. They converged on the shopping plaza in an alarming visual that scared the crap out of me. My nightmare was transpiring before my eyes. I assumed this was a sting targeting me and my crew. *I'm going to jail*, I realized. The pizza place was surrounded. I didn't know what to do. My heart raced, palms sweaty, and I don't mean like Eminem. I knew how serious this was. Could this be the end of the road? And not like Boyz II Men.

A police officer entered the pizza parlor. His eyes were fixated on me. *Oh my God, it's over*, I thought. *There's no way I'm getting out of this.*

He addressed me. "What are you doing in here?" he asked.

I offered my best confused face and replied, "Getting a slice of pizza." Like, *duh, what else?*

He continued examining me. Finally, after what felt like a lifetime, and to my complete shock and dismay, he turned away. He walked out of the pizza place. I have no idea why, but he just…walked out, leaving me with my racing thoughts and heart.

I collected myself, shifted the Sicilian corner slice dripping grease down my wrists, then slowly exited the parlor as nonchalantly as possible.

When I reached fresh air, adrenaline spiked as my worst fears were realized. My eyes widened at the sight of my cousin bent over the back of a cop car, hands cuffed behind his back. He saw me and called out, "That's my cousin! He drove me here!"

I looked around as if I had no idea who he was or what he was talking about.

"Nah, man. I have no idea who this dude is," I told another cop staring intently at me. "I'm just here to get a slice."

He looked at me for another second or two as my fate hung in the balance. "Let him go," the cop said.

I exhaled before walking as innocently but briskly as possible around the back of the shopping center, where my car was parked next to a dumpster. I thew my slice in it. Confirming I was out of sight, I next opened my trunk. Took out the remaining prescription pads. Ran over to the dumpster while pulling a lighter out of my pocket. After another glance around to verify the coast was clear, I lit the pads on fire, fanning the flames until the edges of charred paper reached my fingers. I then threw the ashes of my remaining prescription pads into the dumpster, jumped in my Bimmer, and raced home. I assumed that would be the police's next stop, and I hoped I would get there in time to sterilize the place.

When I got home, I told Lauren what had happened. She was shook. I was shook. Beyond shook. It was the last straw for us both. I had nearly been arrested with multiple stolen books of prescription pads, not to mention whatever narcotics I had on my person. I would have gone to prison if fate hadn't had other plans for me.

Something had to change. I knew I needed serious help. My addiction had turned scary for us both, and we didn't know how to deal with it. And now, to compound matters, the forged scripts caper was over. My access to unlimited inventories of pills was gone. Very soon, I knew I would be deathly ill. The jig was up.

Within a week, all my stuff was in storage. Lauren and I broke up, sharing a teary-eyed, bittersweet goodbye while I boarded a plane to Florida.

I was going to rehab. For the first time.

CHAPTER 7

REHAB (#1)

I didn't walk—I ran—to rehab after the pizza parlor debacle. It wasn't even a conversation; it was understood by everyone that this was what Mike needed. My life was in shambles, everything a total collapse. The only positive was that when Lauren and I broke up before I left, it was on good terms. Our separation wasn't because we didn't love each other. It was because my life had become unmanageable. I was physically sick all the time. I embraced risky behaviors to feed my habit. I had no job, no career path. I had no money. If I went twenty-four hours without consuming significant amounts of prescription opiates, I became violently ill. Addiction had snuck up on me and smacked me over the head with a frying pan. Now I had to figure out how to pick myself up.

The answer seemed simple to me: go to rehab and get professional help detoxing. After, I would be good as new...at least I thought. Writing that now, I realize how ridiculous that supposition was, but back then, I had no education or knowledge about recovery. But at least I wasn't stupid enough to go about it on my own. I knew I needed medical assistance to come off opiates. The problem was I had no money for rehab. This was around the time of my parents' divorce, and the family was fractured. Collectively, we seemed disjointed. A lot of strained relationships, people not talking to each other. But when I experienced this crisis, it was like, "Okay, something's happening with Michael," and it was all hands on deck. A 9-1-1 situation for the family. Everyone chipped in to help when I was down and out.

Starting with my brother Marc. On brand for the straight-A student who always had his shit together, Marc had become a success flipping properties. One of Marc's principles was to never give money to family, a lesson I would eventually absorb as good policy, but when I needed it most, Marc stepped up financially. He offered to pay for me to go to rehab. I don't know how much it cost him, but I know it wasn't cheap.

He probably put up somewhere in the neighborhood of ten to twenty thousand dollars for me to go. It was very generous of him; I was very grateful then, and I'm very grateful now.

My dad had moved to Florida and agreed to take me to the facility and let me stay with him after I was released. A few days after escaping what felt like a police sting at the pizza parlor, I boarded a plane with a ticket purchased by my brother, with just enough oxycodone to get me to rehab hidden in an Advil bottle in my toiletry bag.

That night, after arriving at my dad's house, I popped whatever pain-killers were left and plopped down to watch a movie, high and living what I thought was my best life. I knew the eight or so Roxicets I had taken would stave off the withdrawals for at least twenty-four hours, and by that time the next day, I would already be a patient at Sunrise Detox in Fort Lauderdale.

At that point, my only goal when doing drugs was to not get sick. I hadn't realized I was physically dependent on these pills until it was too late. Early on, I'd noticed headaches or cold sweats when I hadn't taken anything for a day or so, but honestly, it never occurred to me that my experimentation was turning into addiction. However, my tolerance increased to such a point that I worked up to averaging ten thirty-milligram oxycodone pills three times a day. Thirty high-powered opiates designed for combating serious pain daily. That's a lot of drugs.

Getting off pills scared me to death. I knew the pain was going to be hell. Whenever I couldn't find pills and started to get sick, I thought I was going to die. Mentally, I was anxious, depressed. I couldn't sleep. Physically, I had the cold sweats. My eyes burned. Skin crawled. Head-ache, stomachache—I just couldn't believe how horrible I felt. And God forbid I went even longer than twenty-four hours without a fix—I'd get so sick, it would be coming out of both ends at the same time.

Have you ever been slumped on the toilet with a trashcan between your legs while shivering and sweating at the same time? I can only hope the answer is no. I wouldn't wish this feeling on my worst enemy. That's why it's so hard for people to get clean. You'll do anything to make that pain go away, to not feel how you currently feel. And you know relief is just a pill away. Making the excruciating pain disappear is just too easy. That's why I knew I needed the professionals to detox me.

The next day, Pops took me to the facility, and I went through the standard intake process. First, I filled out a questionnaire, being honest about the drugs I'd done in my life and what substances were currently in my body. They gave me a piss test to confirm, then conducted a bag check. I was clean. I'd already consumed all the drugs I had remaining the previous night. Next, they set me up in a pretty standard room with a bed and TV. I settled in and prepared to start feeling like shit.

The next day, as the drugs wore off, that's exactly what happened, and I alerted the staff to my worsening condition. They responded by providing me with probably anywhere from an eight- to sixteen-milli-gram dose of Suboxone, a drug used to treat opioid addiction that eases withdrawal symptoms. (Later, I would be hired as a spokesman for the drug.) Over the next week to ten days, the facility's doctors and nurses continued administering Suboxone, lowering the dosage each time, until finally, I was taking only a single milligram a day. Then, nothing.

You still don't feel great the first few days after coming completely off all substances. That's when the journey to get back to your baseline begins. Back to who you were before the drugs. It takes time to get there, often a lot of time, something else I wasn't aware of back then.

Getting clean from substances is like traveling a bridge that takes you back to real life. It's a long, scary, wobbly bridge filled with missteps and treachery. You need patience and dedication to traverse it. You've been on an island separated from reality by the drugs for so long that when the chemicals leave your body, it's a painful trip back to reality.

Look at it this way: For however long you've been in active addiction, you've been high. In a fog. Those painkillers desensitize you, prevent you from feeling life, from feeling your raw emotions. Once you detox, as you get back to your baseline, all those buried emotions rush back to the surface. A lot of people don't understand what's happening when those feelings come barreling back. I know I didn't that first go-around. The anxiety and depression all hit you at once, and it really sucks. But each day, little by little, everything begins to subside. There is no easy fix, no cure-all to make it go away. All you can do is abstain from narcotics, exercise, hydrate, get sunlight, and embrace good old-fashioned Mother Earth. When all else fails, you just have to do the next right thing. Put one foot in front of the other to move forward. Eventually, you'll get there. I promise.

Many people don't have the patience to endure that journey, and that's a big reason why they relapse. They think *this is taking too long* or aren't willing to tolerate the pain. I believe a lot of people think that pain is a bad thing, and I disagree. I think it's the opposite. It's better to embrace the pain. Pain in life is inevitable, and you can't ignore it. Drugs bury it. They don't make it go away. When you get sober, all that recessed pain is dug up. You have to work through it to get back to your baseline. Life doesn't get easier; you get stronger.

So that's what I did in rehab. Or at least attempted to do. I medically detoxed with professional help, then spent the next thirty days at their inpatient rehab center. I graduated after completing the thirty-day program but didn't have the right mindset—not then. I was young, I was uneducated, and I just figured *these guys are going to fix me*. I didn't yet understand the immense amount of work it takes to truly get and stay sober.

Sure, I was going through the motions. I went to the sessions. I shared during group. But I didn't take it as seriously as I should have. Similar to how I tackled most things in my life at the time, I coasted in rehab. I didn't think I was like those other people. They had sold their kitchen cabinets for crack. That wasn't me. I had to stay away from these pills, yeah, but I was youthful. I was resilient. And I wasn't ready to stop partying. I wasn't hanging up my player's jersey anytime soon.

Besides, I thought I was cured. A laughable statement to anyone in the recovery community, but again, I still didn't understand what it meant to be clean and sober and how many different ways you have to fight. It isn't just about physically detoxing—you have to mentally detox too. To get rid of bad habits and educate yourself on how to behave, how to replace negative habits with positive ones.

But I had no idea about any of this. I simply believed if I just stopped taking opiates, I'd be fine. I never considered I shouldn't drink or party. I wanted to get back out there and find Mrs. Right. Lauren and I had broken up on good terms and still talked, but she had moved on with her life. It was time I did the same.

CHAPTER 8

THE SITUATION FINDS INSPIRATION

Hopefully I've properly articulated how our breakup did not stem from a lack of love or even troubles in the relationship. It was more so because I was sick. When I was using drugs, the fog surrounding me meant that I couldn't focus on being a good partner. But even after breaking up, Lauren and I remained close. The chains of addiction and dependency couldn't dissipate the bond we shared.

Once detox concluded and I settled into life at the treatment facility, Lauren and I began talking on the phone each day. She was living her life—no, excelling at life—in New York City while I was…in here. I accepted the fact that we were no longer together and knew things had happened the way they were supposed to, but I also believed that if you let a bird out of the cage and it came back, it was meant to be. And I knew I wanted Lauren to come back. She encompassed everything I looked for in a woman. She was Italian, cute, smart, and assertive and came from a good family with the same values as mine. We enjoyed a mutual respect and love. I needed to demonstrate to her that I was The One; I had no doubt she was for me. I was going to prove my worthiness as a partner to her or die trying. Staying clean would be the first step.

As I worked through rehab and got up to speed on Lauren's new life without me, I gained even more respect for her. She had picked up the pieces of a life that my mistakes had shattered and moved back in with her parents. Now she was attacking her dreams. I was locked down in a rehabilitation center, talking to her on the phone while she was on the train going into Manhattan, interning for Ferragamo and attending fashion school in the city. Just crushing it.

We talked about getting back together, but Lauren was rightfully skeptical and hesitant. She was thriving on her own. I think there was a concern I could jeopardize her progress.

That hurt to think about, but hearing about the things she was accomplishing was so inspiring. She motivated me. Here was this girl I had dated for four years, my college sweetheart whom I loved with all my heart, and she was going for it. It lit a fire in me. I decided then and there that when I got out of rehab, I was going to work my ass off and turn my dreams into reality. For Lauren. For us.

We've already established my best asset is my body. That was going to be my ticket to stardom. This time, I wanted to utilize my shredded body while keeping my clothes on. Well, most of them at least.

While in the facility, I reverted to leaning on fitness as a coping mechanism. I was the kid up at six every morning, running through the neighborhoods of south Florida with a sweatshirt on while everyone else was snug under the covers in their room. Using my pain as fuel. I was upset that I had put myself in here and let a substance get the best of me. I was devastated that the love of my life was moving on without me. It hurt knowing my family was disappointed in me. Countless pushups, pullups, and calisthenics pushed the pain out.

Once I got out of rehab, I hit the gym even harder. Most people thought I was crazy with the amount I was working out, but that was just my OCD kicking in. Obsession is the common thread in everything I do. It's in my DNA. It was responsible for turning me into a drug addict, but now I was exploiting it for good. Nurturing that passion allowed me to get back in peak physical shape in no time. I was determined to be a physical specimen and put my best foot forward to break into the entertainment world.

After rehab, I moved in with my father in Delray Beach. He mandated that while living in his home I had to have a job, so I waited tables while spending most of my time working out, partying, and trying to get girls. I stayed away from pills, but that didn't mean I was suddenly on the path to success. I still had this vague desire to break into show business, but I needed direction and structure.

Pops recognized my lack of motivation all too well. There was an incident where he found a couple pounds of weed hidden in the ceiling of the basement. After confirming a buyer, I came home to pick up some weight. But when I pulled the tiles back, I found the space in the ceiling vacant. My stomach dropped as I realized exactly what had transpired. I called my father.

"Did you by chance find something of mine?" I asked.

"I did," he answered. "And now it's mine."

"Yours? I need that back."

"You can't be selling drugs in my home. There are consequences."

"What are the consequences?" I asked.

"You have to buy it back from me."

"I don't have the money to buy it back," I said, now starting to get really worried. "If I don't have the money for my dealer, it's going to be a serious problem for me."

"Don't care. Not my problem," he answered.

After I pleaded with him for a while, we finally came to an agreement. He'd return the weed for a percentage of the sale. I was fine with the deal and had to chuckle. I knew this was the old man's way of teaching me a lesson. But it wasn't the first time something similar had happened. My dad was rightly fed up with me.

One day not long after, he sat me down and delivered an ultimatum:

"You're too wild," he started. "You've always been uncontrollable and anti-authority, but I've had enough. I'm kicking you out. You have two weeks. After that, I'm driving you down to the recruiter's office, and you're joining the military. The only one who can straighten you out is Uncle Sam."

And that was that. My dad drove me to the navy recruiter. I took the entrance exam, got high scores, and subsequently planned on joining the navy. I figured I'd do the military thing for a few years, then get out and be a firefighter. That's exactly what my dad wanted, and I guess I thought it was what I wanted too.

I had two weeks left before signing on the dotted line. I couldn't help but feel like I was being forced into the decision. I had never responded well to being told I *had* to do something. Doubts started to creep in, and I wondered if the military truly was my fate. Was I shortchanging my future?

Lauren continued to inspire me with all the impressive things she was doing with her life. My greatest fear was being left behind by her. I couldn't shake this feeling that I was wasting my potential and there was more for me in this world than the military or a firehouse. Not that there is anything wrong with either of those options—they are both honorable professions that afford many of my friends from my hometown a great life while helping others. But I knew even then that I was a star. I just needed the right people to see me shine. I would never forgive myself if I didn't follow in Lauren's footsteps and follow my own dreams. I had to throw this Hail Mary and see if I had what it took.

So I decided to leave my destiny in the hands of the Almighty. I had two weeks to try. If this last gasp failed, I would accept my father's plan and go into the navy. If nothing else, the ultimatum had delivered the motivation I required to finally take action.

I mentioned how everyone always told me I needed to do something with my body. But now, they were saying it to me in the past tense. Like my time had come and gone. Hell, I was only twenty-five years old! Their doubt fertilized my resolve—if anyone thought I was past my prime, they had another thing coming. I was going to go for it. I wasn't going to get left behind. I was in the best shape of my life. It was time to capitalize on it.

I asked some girl I was dating at the time to take photos of me in my underwear—no shirt, backwards hat, Calvin Kleins rising from sagging jeans. You best believe I used one of those images as my Myspace profile picture! The reaction I got anytime someone saw me with my shirt off made me think I could do a Calvin Klein campaign like Mark Wahlberg (a campaign that would be offered to me a few years later). My abs were better than those on any underwear box, and I figured I could get some male modeling gigs. After Googling "fitness and underwear modeling agencies in New York," I sent three photos out to the first five search results. Then, as the clock ticked down, I waited.

I didn't have to wait long. Within three days, I heard back from three of the agencies I'd queried. Now, don't get me wrong—these weren't high-end agencies. Ford or Elite they were not. But their desire to add me to their roster so quickly was validation. It meant I was on the right path. *My* path. My father's way was the safe path. I had never followed the safe path. In life, when the chips are down, I always bet on myself. It was time to go all in.

Hopefully I've done an adequate job of describing my father's personality for you to predict his reaction when I told him I no longer planned on joining the military and instead was going to be an underwear model. It wasn't laughter, per se, more like, "Suit yourself. You're on your own now, kid."

And I was. Without a job, an income, anywhere to go, or anywhere to live, I headed back to Jersey, where I couch-surfed for a while before finally moving in with my brother Frank and his wife. There was no plan B. I signed with one of those rinky-dink modeling agencies, and so began the effort to book modeling gigs for, I don't know, the underwear section of the JCPenney catalogue or something. We're not talking a runway in Paris, but it was good enough for me. Getting signed was a small step in the right direction that proved I had what it took. I wasn't drug dealing, I wasn't taking pills, and a sense of purpose seemed to be growing. Somehow, I knew deep in my soul that this was going to work out.

To celebrate my male modeling contract, in typical guido fashion, me and the boys went down to the shore. Seaside, specifically. As we walked the streets, I remember feeling excited and validated about this new life trajectory. As we got closer to the club, I undid more buttons on my shirt in preparation to unveil my best asset. The way my physique was put together, I knew my best outfit was nothing. By the time we reached the entrance, my shirt was fully parted, and people were taking notice.

One woman in particular called out, "Oh my God, look at his abs. That's a situation!" My buddies began to chuckle, and we all looked at the speaker, a young woman holding hands with another man. She was pointing at me, mouth agape. To my surprise, her boyfriend looked like he agreed with her. I laughed and said, "Nah, that's not a situation; this is *the* situation," and I pointed at my abs, flexing while everyone smiled and laughed.

And that, ladies and gentlemen, is how The Situation was born.

More than a year later, MTV called me in to do a final interview after they officially picked the show up. As I took my chair, I looked around at the producers who would be interviewing me.

"I'm more comfortable with my shirt off," I said, lifting my tight tee overhead. "You don't mind, do you?" Bare chested, I smirked at the room and ignored the sea of shocked expressions.

With my audience properly dismayed, we got down to the interview. The producers began by asking my name and if I had a nickname.

"Yeah," I said. "They call me Mikey Abs."

The interviewer didn't look impressed. "Mikey Abs? Do you have anything better?"

I leaned back in my seat. "Actually, I do." I proceeded to tell them the story about that night on the boardwalk, and they were enthralled. "That *is* a situation!" one of them exclaimed.

"You know what? That's my name. The Situation," I said.

"That's brilliant!" the interviewer responded. "Do you have that trademarked?"

I quickly nodded and assured them that indeed I did. The second I left that meeting, the first thing I did was Google "how to trademark a name" and started the application process immediately.

Before all that, right after getting signed to the modeling agency, I began to attend "go-sees" all over Manhattan. However, after three months, I still wasn't booking any modeling jobs. I looked ridiculous, completely shredded, to where the casting directors thought my abs were photoshopped in my portfolio, but somehow it didn't lead to landing any gigs.

These casting calls had a weird energy. Most of the photographers were male, and they kept trying to hang out with me after the photo shoots. They'd ask if they could take me to dinner or if I wanted to go to their Hamptons house with them. I was like, "Nah, I'm good." Being new to the business, I just thought that was how this industry went. I do remember seeing some of the other guys on the roster getting booked, and I couldn't figure out why. Still, I remained optimistic and steadfast in my belief that I'd get a break.

Then, one day, I saw a flyer tacked to the wall at one of these go-sees. "Casting Call for the Hottest Guidos and Guidettes," it read. *Oh, shit. That's me!* It seemed like fate calling. The event was to take place in Atlantic City at The Pool at Harrah's. *Oh, hell yeah. I'll be there.*

On the day of the casting call, I showed up at Harrah's with my club crew and trademark confidence. The place was stocked with the best-looking, most in-shape Italians from the tri-state area—and then there was me, who looked like my abs had been created in a lab. Amongst all these specimens, I was a clear cut above. Even though everyone in attendance was young and good-looking, me and my crew considered ourselves the A team. I was our secret weapon. Just tell The Situation to lift his shirt up and watch the crowd and cameras come running.

Upon checking in and entering the pool area, we were greeted by a sea of fist-pumping guidos, most of them jacked up on MDMA, GHB, alcohol, and testosterone. Circles of dance battles broke out around us like self-combusting forest fires. The familiar Jersey Shore fragrance of sweat, spray tan, and cologne filled our nostrils as laser lights shined off bouncing gold chains. Hissing fog machines lending a surreal visual quality completed this frantic scene.

Now this was a party! It was the natural habitat of the hottest creatures in the New York metro area, and we were the alpha dogs. We roamed the grounds like a dominant wolf pack on the hunt, sniffing and marking our territory as we scavenged prey.

An extremely attractive girl wearing a yellow dress and holding a clipboard picked her way through the masses, scouting the animated revelers like a mobile bikini contest judge as every contestant attempted to gain her attention and favor. (I ended up dating her for a while after this.) Clipboard girl worked for the casting company, and her job was to find the complete package of looks, charm, and charisma that would grab America's attention. She took notes as she perused and conversed with the natives: "Beautiful but airhead." "Would be horrible on TV." "Epitome of what we're looking for" (that last one was about me).

They knew what type of characters would make this show a hit and how to find them, even if most of us in attendance only had some vague idea that we were participating in a general call for a VH1 show billed as "America's Top Guido." The majority of the attendees were just there to party, and no one was disappointed; it was a hell of a party. The producers were all over me during the event, so I wasn't surprised when a week later, I got a call from clipboard girl.

"You're exactly what we're looking for," she told me. "We want to make a sizzle reel of you."

Cool, I thought. *What's a sizzle reel?*

Anthony Beltempo, Jersey Shore *co-creator:*

I had this idea for a show about guidos. I grew up on the Jersey Shore and I knew the guido lifestyle—heck, I'm half a guido myself. It's a fascinating subculture that I wanted to tell the world about because they're so outrageous yet so endearing at the same time. That's not a common mix, but it is a very interesting one.

I took the idea to VH1, and they gave me a very small budget to go shoot a demo tape, or sizzle. I got together with an awesome casting director named Mike Petolino, and we went in search of the type of people who would make this show a hit. People who had the looks, the attitude, and the personality. We each grew up with and knew a million kids similar to what we were looking for, but the trick would be finding those guidos and guidettes with the intangibles that would enthrall America.

Mike Petolino started by hitting up all the big clubs down the shore. He'd set up a table and pass out questionnaires with outrageous questions on it like, "Rank what's most important to you: how white your teeth are; how tan you are; how tight your hair looks; how vascular you are." We knew how the people we wanted for the show would answer. Hordes of them came up to fill out this questionnaire in these loud clubs. I'm pretty sure most people didn't even know what they were filling out, but it was like, *Hey, it's a shot at something. I'll participate.* We ended up with thousands and thousands of completed questionnaires, each one with a Polaroid photo of the responder attached.

I remember looking at Mike Sorrentino's. His picture looked great—visually, he was exactly what we were looking for. I believe he was holding his shirt up in the photo, showing off his abs, sunglasses perched on the tip of his nose even though it was nighttime and indoors. All his answers were very creative and funny. Before even meeting him, Mike Sorrentino had separated himself from the pack and was a frontrunner for the show.

After reviewing these piles of questionnaires, my colleagues and I narrowed it down to a small group of people whom we wanted to film demo tapes with to see how they looked and acted on camera. We decided to follow these four people around with a small camera crew one weekend down the shore while they went about the things guidos do to maintain their look and lifestyle: go to the barber shop, work out at the gym, pre-game at the shore house they were renting, hit the bars, then go back to the house for late night.

I remember that Saturday night, I tagged along with Mike Sorrentino and a guy called Joey Fist Pumps, real name Joey DeSalvo, who's almost like the fifth Beatle. Joey Fist Pumps got selected for the show but declined because he was offered a union job in construction. After the success of season one, he wanted to come back, but by then, it was too late.

That first night, I had my camera and was going back and forth between Mike the Situation and Joey Fist Pumps at a packed Headliners in Neptune. These two were the life of the party. Every girl was coming up to them; every guy was watching them. It was a show. Mike kept lifting his shirt up, and like moths to a flame, girls would flock to him. I mean, he was a great-looking guy, and combine that with the huge biceps, the abs, and the camera following him around, of course you're going to get tons of women approaching.

"I put the 'V' in VH1," he said for probably the hundredth time as yet another tanned bleach blond lifted his shirt up and rubbed those freakish abs before triple kissing him with her friend.

Mike was a good sport about it all. A natural. He was very easy to work with, and he just kept dropping these lines that were gold. I remember at one point that weekend, as we were filming him driving, he had one hand on the steering wheel when he turned casually toward the camera. Out of the blue and with absolutely no context, he eloquently stated, "I mean, what are you gonna do when a guy takes off his shirt and he pretty much looks like Rambo?"

I have no idea why he said it, but it was such a random, laughable moment that we loved and seemed to encapsulate Mike. Only he could be that arrogant but at the same time possess the self-awareness to be in on the joke. He got it. He didn't take himself too seriously. The guy oozed with confidence, but he had humility too.

The weekend of filming concluded. I didn't even need to see the footage to know that Mike was a shoo-in for the show. Once we showed the sizzle to VH1, they agreed. They loved him. We knew we were sitting on gold.

CHAPTER 9

GREEN LIT

This show *had* to work out. The Situation was running out of options. I'd recently completed rehab. I was off pills and no longer drug dealing, which was great, but that also meant I had no income. I wasn't doing the modeling anymore because honestly, the photographers were just trying to bang me every time I went to a casting call. I had retired from stripping. I'd decided against joining the military. I had no interest in going back to school. There were no other career prospects on the horizon. I had no backup plan. *I* was the backup plan. At the time, all I had to my name was seven dollars and a six-pack.

What I also had was tunnel vision. All my energy and focus became directed at breaking into the entertainment industry, specifically this unnamed guido show I'd been offered but that hadn't been picked up yet. They were calling it "America's Next Top Guido" or "America's Biggest Guido" at the time, and it was supposed to be a competition show. That's all I knew about it—well, that and I planned to use it as a launchpad to stardom. However, I was the only one who believed that. You have to give me credit—I had the balls to go after my ambitions and the confidence to stick with the vision even when everyone around me was telling me to give up my chance at fame and get a real job.

"You have to get serious about your life," Mom constantly nagged as I waited for the show to move forward. "You're looking for that needle in a haystack. It's a very unattainable goal, and the odds are against you."

My father was of the same mindset and expressed similar concerns, doing so with even more volume. Not trying to besmirch Papa Sorrentino here, but he was still pushing me to be a firefighter or get a union job right up until the first episode of *Jersey Shore* aired. At no point did he believe superstardom was my future.

"You're wasting your time," he always told me. "This path you're on is going nowhere. You gotta get a job, pay bills. We all know you have amazing abs, but there are millions of people with amazing abs."

I didn't agree with that. I possessed the belief that I was one of a kind and destined for greatness. I remained resolute in my path.

Still, in some sense, I knew they were right. This was the longest of shots. Like all good parents, they wanted their son to take the safe route. But I had this gut feeling that I had found my calling with reality TV and something special was about to happen. Fate seemed to be whispering to me. I had to play this out, or I would never forgive myself. So while I didn't blame my family for not having faith, I never lost hope. I knew this show was going to get picked up and be huge.

That belief in myself was easy to embrace—I knew what we had on film. I saw the character I had portrayed while under the camera's hot lights when filming the sizzle reel for VH1. I was a natural. Sometimes, when people are on camera, they shrink. They depict a side of themselves that is not flattering. That wasn't me. I was like a plant under the sun, rising to the light. My true self came out when the cameras were rolling, and the lines effortlessly flowing from my mouth were TV gold. I possessed the "it" factor that would undoubtably make this show a smash hit. Which is why, through those months and months of uncertainty, waiting to hear if it had been picked up, I remained self-assured and positive my hopes and dreams were going to come to fruition.

Another shimmering light had re-entered my world since I had completed rehab and gotten off pills, and that was Lauren. As I said, we never stopped talking or, really, loving each other since breaking up. In fact, I had invited her to the club when we filmed the sizzle reel, but just as a friend. She was not entertained in the least watching her ex-boyfriend make out with random girls as they licked whipped cream off his stomach. Lauren was classy and didn't flock to the bright lights. In fact, after watching from a distance that night, she let me know that I had acted like a jackass. In my defense, we were both single, and I was doing nothing wrong. Now, if she wanted to get back together, that could all change...

As we continued to navigate our complicated friendship, I remained impressed with all the great things that she was doing. Her growth was what had made me want to do more with my life. She was a big reason why I was working so hard to get this show made. Lauren was why I wanted to be a success.

While I waited to see if the show would get picked up, our conversations turned to potentially getting back together. We were both ready to make this work. Though each of us were dating other people, there was an understanding that we were each other's great loves. But the prospect of this show threatened all that. Lauren made it clear that if I did the show, we couldn't be together. She didn't want to be the girl at home crying while her boyfriend was on some reality show acting a fool. And she was a million percent right. I had a big choice to make: do the show or get back with Lauren.

I didn't have to make any decisions right away. The thing was, not a whole lot of progress had been made since that weekend filming almost a year earlier with Anthony Beltempo. Yeah, the producers told me that I was exactly what they were looking for and that they planned to create a reality show around me, but it still hadn't been sold to a network.

To Anthony's credit, he called me regularly to ease any doubt about the show's validity. "Don't worry," he'd say during each month's phone call. "Everyone loves you. This is the normal process. It takes a while for a show to get picked up. We're still trying to find the right cast members to complement you. The show is going to happen. Keep being patient."

That was good enough for me. As I said, I knew what we had. More importantly, *I* knew *they* knew what we had. Still, it was getting more difficult to answer everyone's questions and keep my parents at bay. I remained broke and unemployed that year while couch-surfing, just waiting for word that the show had been picked up and my dreams had come true.

Finally, that day came. My gamble had paid off, as I knew it would.

I remember getting the call like it was yesterday. I was with my sister in her Infiniti G35. We had just had dinner at my mom's house and were sitting in her car talking. Deadmau5's "I Remember" was on the radio when my phone rang. Anthony. I picked up. Immediately, I was over-taken by the excitement in his voice.

"It's official!" he exclaimed. "We did it! The show was picked up by MTV! Get ready for your life to change."

For maybe the first time in my life, I was speechless. Time seemed to slow down as this life-altering news sank in. I could feel the hair stand up across my body. This was it. My prayers had been answered. When I hung up, I had quarters in my pocket but tears in my eyes.

I turned to my sister and told her what had happened. Knowing I was broke, she did something amazing that I'll always be grateful for and that I'm proud to have been able to repay many times over. Since I would need clothes for the show, Melissa offered to buy me a new ward-robe. Everything was coming together.

Unfortunately, there was a downside to the good news. Life has a funny sense of humor, but I also believe everything happens for a reason. Ironically, this long-awaited arrival of my first real opportunity at break-ing into show business simultaneously torpedoed any chance of recon-ciling with Lauren. We were like two ships passing in the night. She wanted stability and a predictable life with a boyfriend who was available. I sought excitement through a risky gamble with what I saw as huge upside potential. I couldn't let this opportunity slip through my fingers.

Once I got the call and told her the show had gotten the green light, Lauren asked if I was going to do it. "I thought we were going to get back together," she said sadly.

"Listen, this is a life-changing opportunity for me. My dream that I've worked so hard for. I don't know what's going to happen, but I have to take this chance."

For a moment, she was quiet. Then she said, "Okay, I get that. But we can't be together while you do the show. If we do, we won't last."

It was bittersweet, but I knew she was 100 percent right. I'm a posi-tive person, and I had hopes that it still could eventually work. Letting a caged bird free and all that. But for now, it was as simple as Lauren being the right person at the wrong time. I had to give her up to follow my dreams. Historically, reality TV and relationships just didn't work. If there was any shot at a reunion, attempting it now would ensure it failed.

It was the best decision we ever made.

CHAPTER 10

WELCOME TO THE SHORE

I showed up to 1209 Ocean Terrace in Seaside Heights, New Jersey, in June of 2009 penniless, jobless, wearing new clothes purchased by my sister, driving a Range Rover owned by my brother. The fresh haircut was my own, and despite not being able to afford those clothes, I had all the confidence in the world in what lay underneath them. I may have arrived at the shore house broke, but also with an eight-pack and unwavering belief in myself.

Funny story: Not only was the Range Rover they filmed me driving from Manalapan to Seaside not my car, but Marc made MTV rent it from him for $500. They needed me to have a vehicle for the travel footage, but I didn't own anything I couldn't carry, let alone a car. I certainly didn't have the five hundred bucks Marc was requesting to use his SUV, so I convinced MTV to pay him for it. They put together a quick contract, and MTV got to film me showing up to the shore house for the first time in a Range Rover rented from my brother.

But there were still some final hoops to jump through before we made it to Seaside. The editing in the first episode makes it seem like we all drove straight from our hometowns to the shore house, but that's not the way it really went down. Before any cast member ever set foot in the house, production put us all up in the Holiday Inn on Route 37 in Toms River. At the time, none of us had any idea who else had been cast in this show and they wanted to keep it that way.

At the hotel, the producers sequestered us so we wouldn't see one another, but I caught them slipping and came across a call sheet. The piece of paper had twelve names and faces on it—including mine, of course—but four were crossed off. I have no idea who those people were, but they ended up cut from the show.

I was like, "Oh, shit!" when I saw their faces x'd out. These were people who had gone through the vetting process and through months

65

of interviews before being told they had been selected to be on this show. They had packed up their lives and come to this Holiday Inn in Toms River to start filming. Or so they thought. Apparently, at the last minute, they had suddenly been told they hadn't made it. Go home. Damn. Cold-blooded.

The remaining cast never really spoke too much about it, but we were all like, "Imagine if you were one of them?"

Of course, I never worried about not being cast. I was the original, the one whom the show had been developed around, so I knew I wasn't in jeopardy. But production wasn't set on the final cast until the last moment when they sat in that hotel tossing names back and forth. Eventually they came up with the perfect dynamic of Snooki, JWoww, The Situation, Pauly D, Vinny, Angelina, Ronnie, and Sammi Sweetheart. The infamous members of *Jersey Shore*.

They worked hard to make sure we never saw each other in that hotel. And they were very strict about the lockdown process. Security checked our bags for drugs or other paraphernalia upon arrival—a process I didn't have to worry about for season one—then kept us in insolation until it was time to leave for the shore house, a process we called "arrivals." We weren't even allowed out of our rooms until departure time, and then they staggered our exits. If there were going to be any meetings or conversations between cast members, they wanted them to be on camera so they could record potential storylines.

If you remember the first episode, they had me arrive at the shore house first. With the camera crew following closely, I left the hotel in Marc's Range Rover, super excited that this day was finally here. After all the work I had put into this, I was finally getting my shot. I had a hard time believing it was even happening but was ultra confident I was going to be the breakout star.

You know when Scarface says, "Who put this thing together? Me, that's who!" It may sound conceited, but that's the way I felt. I was the only one who had filmed the pilot. I was the main reason why MTV had bought the show. I'd been the first one cast, over a year ago. Production had been telling me the search for the remaining roommates was based on them complementing me. I didn't tell the others that, but in my brain, I was like, *This thing was put together by me.* I definitely felt a sense of ownership for the show and was going to do everything I could to make sure it was a hit and I was front and center.

That's why I had such a presence that first season. It was almost like I had a chip on my shoulder, where I was looking for validation or appreciation for being the catalyst that made this all happen. I felt responsible for the show and therefore a leader, the alpha in the house. The others went through a completely different casting experience based on the personality I'd provided the production company a year earlier. So I definitely felt like the man. I was ready to be the king of Seaside and have the summer of my life.

When you're from Jersey, it's a rite of passage to go down the shore during the summer. You get a house with your friends and you live and work and party for the summer at the beach. It's all about the weekends at the shore. All week, you prep for the weekend. You go tanning, go to the gym, and get your outfits ready for Friday, Saturday, and Sunday. It's an adventure. That adventure was what the show was all about. I knew with cameras and a film crew beside me, the sky was the limit.

I hadn't partied much in Seaside previously. Seaside was known as where the younger crowds usually hung out—prom parties and such. My crew from home usually tore it up in Belmar and Point Pleasant, which honestly, were a cut above Seaside. That's where the good-looking people went. But the castmates and I had the mentality of, *Okay, these are the cards we were dealt; we're gonna have to bring the people to Seaside.* Eventually, that's exactly what happened.

When I first pulled up to the house, I thought the outside looked nice. It was in a great location, close to the boardwalk and beach. I thought it had great energy. The roof was amazing. But the inside... How do I say this nicely? The inside was a little dated. A little used. I didn't think it was that nice. As I said, my houses in Belmar and Point Pleasant were more respectable. But that was alright—I was determined to make the most of it.

In the meantime, I explored my new home for the summer and waited for the other castmates to show up. It was almost like the first day of school when you're excited to see the other attractive people in your class. I couldn't wait to see who else was going to be a part of this unknown reality show.

Pauly was the first one to arrive after me. When he walked in the door, I was like, *Aight, we cool. This is gonna be good.* He and I immediately clicked. I mean, his name is Paul Michael; mine is Michael Paul. My birthday is July 4; his is July 5. He's a good-looking guy; I'm a good-looking guy. We both dressed great and were the same height. Both tan. Both jacked. He had a natural swag I recognized in myself. I knew that with us together, it was going to be an epic summer.

The other guys seemed good too. It was a good-looking crew, which was important. Ronnie struck me as being built like a pit bull—short and stocky. I still joke with him to this day that he has no neck. I liked him but sensed right off the bat we would have a problem at some point. Anytime testosterone-fueled alphas reside in close quarters while drinking alcohol, it's a foregone conclusion something's going to happen.

I could tell Vinny was that typical mama's boy from Staten Island, the type of kid who didn't like pretty boy guidos like me. He didn't quite fit the same mold as me, Pauly, and Ronnie. He was pale and not in shape. Had no interest in GTL'ing. Vinny graduated from college and had been studying to be a lawyer before the show. Honestly, he seemed like the odd man out. Maybe he was a diversity hire, I don't know, haha.

JWoww walked in with a jug of protein. I thought she kind of looked like a fitness model with a don't-fuck-with-me club promoter vibe. Jenni was immediately able to mesh with both the girls and the guys, going back and forth to foster a connection with all of us. She was like the mother hen of the house. And boy, if you fucked with one of her chicks, there would be hell to pay. Or potentially a spinning back fist.

When Nicole walked in, the first thing I thought was *damn, the party is here!* Definitely loud. Maybe fiery is a better way to describe Snooki back then. She looked like a little chihuahua, you know what I mean? Cute and short in stature, but that girl could drink you under the table. Snooki was like the Energizer Bunny, keeping the party alive until the wee hours of the morning, outlasting everyone. She made her presence felt right off the bat, as evidenced by the first episode when she got wasted. That night happened exactly as it played out on TV. No scripts or cute editing. I'm certainly glad she stayed, and we've developed a lifelong friendship.

Then, there was Angelina. Ah, Angelina. Little-known fact: I knew Angelina already. We'd actually hooked up a couple of times back in the day when we both were in the same club scene. In fact, when Anthony Beltempo asked me during the casting process if I knew anyone else who would be good for the show, I referred and vouched for Angelina. Before the show, we got along really well. During the casting process, she always texted me each time she made it to the next interview and let me know prior to arriving in Seaside that she had been cast. Still, when she first walked in the door, I was like *wow, she really did make it.*

Right off the bat, I could tell Angelina was a different person on camera. I mean, I knew the girl. I knew how she was. Instead of acting like her normal self, she became extra and confrontational. Maybe it was a coping mechanism when the cameras were rolling. I've always said I'm the same guy on camera as I am in person. I don't have different masks. Angelina clearly did, and I didn't like that. I don't know if I should admit this or not, but the Kim Kardashian of Staten Island wouldn't exist if it weren't for me.

While Deena didn't join the show until season three as Angelina's replacement, she quickly became part of the family. My first impression of Deena was that this was a fun, unpredictable ball of energy. A blast in a glass. She was the perfect Robin to Snooki's Batman. Together, those two meatballs could drink us all under the table.

I actually knew Sammi a little bit before the show too. We used to hang out with the same crew, but it was more like a "hi and bye" relationship when we saw each other out. When she arrived, I thought she was a cute girl. Obviously, we were vibing in the beginning of the show, but she ended up getting with Ronnie.

In the end, that was a good thing for me. I didn't want anything serious during the show. A wise man once said, "Never fall in love at the Jersey Shore." I knew I was on a wild ride, and a girlfriend would only slow me down. I was looking for adventure and the thrill of the unknown, not to get wifed up. To become a legend, a story, a larger-than-life character. I couldn't do that tied down. There was no way I was going to lock myself up while all this was going on. Heroes come and go, but legends never die.

And that was the cast. The rest is history.

CHAPTER 11
MAKING A SHOW

After filming concluded that summer, I left the shore house with actual goosebumps. I was so proud and optimistic about what we had just completed that a tingling sensation ran throughout my entire body as I steered Marc's once-again rented Range Rover back home to sleep on friends' and family's couches while waiting for the show to air. I had no doubt that once it did, superstardom would be my fate.

It had been a magical summer. Just a phenomenal moment in my young life, which I had taken full advantage of. If Lauren was the right girl at the wrong time for Mike, Seaside had been the right place at the right time for The Situation. And I had shown the right attitude in seizing this opportunity.

I was convinced we had just filmed something never seen before. That what the eight of us had done in Seaside that summer would change the face of reality TV forever. The surreal moments and the hookups and the fights—I knew America would be mesmerized by our characters once they had a chance to view the show. Though no one had seen so much as a single frame yet, I already felt like the cock of the walk. In my head, I was a superstar. The problem was, until the damn show was on TV, the only person who knew it was me.

After that first season wrapped, we all went back to normal life. Everything show-related simply fizzled out. We'd shot this amazing season of reality television, but we didn't know when, or honestly if, it would air. As the leaves changed that fall, we saw no promos, no coming attractions, nothing. To everyone back home, I was the same old Mike, just back from a summer of partying in Seaside. *Oh, a camera crew followed you around? Cool.* No one else knew about the amazing content we had just created.

And I knew that it *had* been amazing. The shore house was almost like college but on steroids. These new roommates turned out to be an incredible dynamic of various personalities that fit together so perfectly that we constantly made spectacular television moments. It was like we were all born to be reality stars. MTV had found a great cast of people just like me. I wasn't the only one who shined under the bright lights. For the most part, all eight of us were unapologetically ourselves and had acted like the cameras weren't even there. That would give America—and the world—an unfiltered look into this guido subculture that they probably didn't even know existed.

Still, meeting a whole new set of people to live, work, and party with while also having cameras on us 24/7 took some adjusting to. The cameras presented a whole litany of challenges that I don't think we anticipated, but we did the best we could navigating this new world.

There was no script or forced storylines. Production never really gave us instructions other than to be ourselves and to do what we normally would do at the shore. So we went tanning. Went to the gym. Prepped our outfits for the night. Went to the club. Drank. Hooked up. Fought. Got mired in crazy escapades. Basically, had the time of our lives. And when you do that with camera crews following, everything gets turned up a notch. YOLO.

Fights were a real problem that summer. Everywhere we went, it was mayhem. Even normally, when you go down the shore, there's a pretty good chance you're going to get in a scuffle. There's a saying down there, "we're either fighting or fucking tonight," and that definitely held true. Usually, both were on the agenda.

When other alphas saw us being filmed and getting all the attention at the clubs, they wanted to test us. That was the way it went. Girls flocked to us, and guys wanted to throw hands. MTV hired security to go out with us, but eight people were doing their own thing and security couldn't be everywhere. Besides, production knew it was good TV if we got in a fight. They wanted to make it real. It always felt like a good ten seconds went by before anyone stepped in to break the fights up. We were the types of people who wouldn't back down, who when faced with "fight or flight" picked the former every single time. All of us threw down that summer, guys and girls. I felt like my head was always on a swivel, waiting for the next guy with an ego who wanted to challenge me.

The people around us seemed to be affected by the cameras more than we were. Take the guy from season one who punched Nicole in the face. If it's been a while since you've watched that episode or if you maybe aren't familiar with the show, yes, a grown man closed-fist punched a tiny female in the face over a shot of tequila. And that guy would never have been around us if not for the cameras.

The proper analogy is that people were drawn to us like moths to a flame. Remember when I said a lot of people change when being filmed? Well, this guy felt his manhood had been questioned and was upset that he had been rejected on camera. That was his ego right there. It was bruised, and the cameras magnified his perceived injuries. I bet that without them, he would have simply walked away rather than assaulting Snooki.

As you can probably imagine, the constant presence of cameras, including ones rigged in the ceilings of our bedrooms, could make it difficult to, shall we say, carry on amorous relations with the opposite sex with any semblance of couth or stealth. We got good at it though. Say one of the guys brought a girl home from the club for a sleepover. We'd say to the girl, "Okay, time to go to sleep," *wink, wink*. And we'd fake being asleep. That was usually good enough to get the cameraman out of the room for the night. But we'd still have to contend with the eye in the sky. That could be overcome by keeping the covers over us both so the cameras couldn't see what was going on under there. We'd build a tent and underneath it do the things consenting adults do.

In some cases, the cameras would come in handy. We always had instant replay available if needed. If there were ever a scenario where someone wanted to say they were encouraged to do something maybe they didn't want to do, production could always go to the tape. And some girls did want to play games, so it was good to know that there was always someone—or something—watching.

And that's the way the summer went. I got to know these new roommates better than I knew anyone outside my own family. Pauly was by far the neatest out of the group, and Angelina was the dirtiest. Ronnie clogged up all the toilets (that was every season). Vinny was always homesick. Nicole was an unpredictable wildcard, and Sam was always straightening her already straight hair. Together, as a group, we were unstoppable and still are to this day.

I implemented Sunday Dinner that first season, and it quickly became an integral part of our story. Food was a big piece of our show. Like any other family, certainly Italian ones, we'd hash out our problems over the dinner table, leaning on our shared heritage. Those dinners brought us together, turned us into a family. Made that house into a home.

Everyone had to be in the kitchen to help. Pauly would set the table while Vinny made the salad. I loved to cook, so I mostly handled that with some help from Jenni. Snooki was supposed to pour the wine but drank most of it instead. Sam and Ron were usually fashionably late, showing up at the dinner table after everything had been served. We'd have to threaten Angelina with exclusion if she didn't chip in.

After dinner, the dishes would always be a thing, piled mountain high in the sink and ignored like the plague. The next day, in between gym, tanning, and laundry, the whole house would pitch in to get them done. Despite all these different personalities, the dinner ritual was very relatable, and I thought America was going to love seeing that.

But as fall went on and we didn't hear anything about the show airing, my insecurities couldn't help but creep in. Had they shelved the whole thing? Fear, doubt, and anxiety reared their ugly heads, and the worst-case scenario played out in my mind.

For months, I had been the positive one, manifesting success for this show. I'd say things like, "I want this to last forever," and people would laugh at me. I didn't blame them—the thought that this was sustainable after filming a single season of unaired reality TV was ludicrous. You're lucky if you get fifteen minutes of fame—but I wanted a lifetime.

From my family's perspective, this dream of famousness was over. It was time for Mike to get back to the real world. To get a job and pay bills and be a productive member of society.

My father had pulled some strings to get me a union job on Staten Island, and I began work as a laborer, a coveted and hard-to-get job. But my heart wasn't in it. The whole time, I was literally daydreaming about being a star. That's right, I was sleeping on the job. I'd find a hiding place to take a nap and fall asleep to dreams about reality stardom. Often, I'd get caught, and the bosses would call my dad and tell him his son was sleeping on the job again. Pops was none too happy with my little siestas and made it clear how hard it had been to get me into the union. The bosses put up with it, I assumed at the time because I was good-looking and charming, but more likely it was probably because of who my father was.

I knew the leniency would only last so long. That's the way it usually went when I had a job—people would put up with me for a while because of my looks and charisma, but eventually, I'd get fired.

I didn't care. While I was grateful for my dad's help, I was lost in a perpetual daydream after leaving the shore. I didn't want to be a union laborer. All I could think about was the show. I refused to let go of my dream.

Finally, we began to hear whispers that a coming attractions trailer was to air. MTV flew me out to California to do press, and it started to feel real again. I walked around with this pep in my step like I was the greatest thing since sliced white bread, even though there hadn't been so much as a preview released yet. My mentality was that if I acted as if the show were already a hit, I could make it so. I stayed steadfast that this unwavering belief in myself would pay off in superstardom. Exuding a positive energy to the world was my way of expressing the results I sought.

Funny story about that first trip to do press: On the flight to California, I joined the mile high club, the first of countless times I got laid because of the show. An attractive girl was sitting in front of me, and we started chatting and flirting. I told her about this new reality show I was in that was about to air and was going to be a smash hit. Even though I wasn't yet a star, just by acting like one, she viewed me as such. She even said that she thought she recognized me from a trailer for the show. I was like, "Honey, I don't know about that. I haven't even seen one. But okay, if you think so…"

We continued to talk, then she gave me a look. You know; a *look*. I returned it. She got up from her seat, glanced at me again, then sauntered down the aisle to the bathroom. I followed. Further details are unrequired.

When we exited the bathroom, the flight attendant shook her head but didn't say anything. My whole life was like that—someone looking at me and telling me not to do something, and then me doing it anyway.

A few months later, I was back in LA and met up with that girl again. This time, Vinny and Pauly were with me. Like Biggie said, I told her, "Tell your friends to get with my friends, and we can be friends." Let's just say she showed up with her two friends, I showed up with my two friends, and we ALL became friends.

I should point out that Lauren and I were still on good but platonic terms at this time, and she was dating someone who she was close to marrying. I was very much single and coming off a summer where it had been my job to hook up with girls. We were in very different places in our lives, to say the least.

After that press junket to California, I began to feel more confident that the show would see the light of day. We were told coming attractions would air during an awards show—I believe it was supposed to be the MTV Video Music Awards. I know all the cast members can relate to this story—we were all so excited to have something tangible to show people. To tell the world, "See? We did this! We created something magical." Each of us made sure that everyone we knew watched that award show, and each of us had our own little viewing party.

I remember Lauren came over to my dad's house in Perth Amboy, and we all sat around, watching this award show, living for the commercials. The ads came and went with no promo for a new reality show about guidos and guidettes. *Hmm. Did we miss it? What the hell is going on?* I didn't know what to tell everyone. It was a deflating moment, for sure, and I know all the cast members felt it.

Then, suddenly, we were given a date for the premiere: December 3, 2009. It was official. We still didn't even know the name of the show at the time, but it was airing! I just hoped it didn't have "guido" in the title. But mostly, I was curious to see how they had edited it, how I looked. I wanted to witness the stories from the previous summer unfold.

I hosted another watch party, this time at Frank's house in Jackson, taking in that first episode of *Jersey Shore* in all its glory with friends, family, and Lauren—this time, without the disappointment and embarrassment at the end. At least from my perspective.

When the show was over, the room was subdued. I was ecstatic, but my family wasn't as optimistic. They didn't want me to do this. I understood where they were coming from. They thought it was just Mike being Mike, only now with cameras on me. They certainly didn't see any potential for what they had just witnessed to be my livelihood. To them, the show airing just meant I was further putting off real life and refusing to mature.

While Lauren wasn't too crazy about watching me hook up with girls on camera, she was happy for me, proud that I was following my dreams despite the high odds of failure. Getting on TV was an accomplishment in itself, but we knew there was no guarantee the show would catch on.

Mostly, I was just relieved it had finally aired. The show was real, and I couldn't help but think that first episode had been epic. I hoped the viewers agreed. I couldn't wait to see the rest.

When the ratings came in, the risk of betting on myself was immediately substantiated and validated. We had a juggernaut. People were watching—millions of them.

It was just the tip of the iceberg. With that premiere of the first episode of *Jersey Shore*, my life changed forever.

CHAPTER 12

A STAR IS BORN

Spring 2010
Miami Beach, Florida

They were onto me. I knew it. This morning, out of the blue, production had suddenly switched up the tanning salons. Ever since season two had started shooting in Miami, we'd been GTL'ing at the same locations. These establishments had been previously vetted and signed the required NDAs and legal documents, and we'd been filming at them since day one. Now, production was suddenly telling us we were going to a different tanning salon? Aw, hell no.

I summoned a bit of that new-celebrity ego I'd been developing and pitched my best mini fit to no avail. When I asked, no one could tell me the reason for the change. I wasn't having it. This was an emergency situation. I *had* to get to the other tanning salon. Time to pivot.

"Okay, cool. We'll go to the new spot. I'll drive," I said, grabbing the keys and jumping in the driver's seat of one of the Escalades we had on standby. To my surprise, Brad, a senior producer, climbed into the shotgun seat. Brad *never* went on location with us. Another red flag indicating the jig was up. But I didn't care. I had a mission to complete, and dammit, I was going to complete it.

We started down the main South Beach drag, ostensibly headed to this new tanning salon where they wanted to film us conducting one of the staples of our daily routine. My Escalade took the lead with Brad in the passenger seat and Jenni, Nicole, Pauly, and Vinny in the back. A production van, two security vehicles, and a cop car completed the caravan. We were rolling deep this morning, an impediment that would make accomplishing my mission that much more difficult.

I wracked my brain as I drove, trying to figure out how I was going to pull this off. I didn't have much time to develop a plan. The old tanning salon, the one I wanted to go to, was coming up on the right. Suddenly, I clutched my midsection and grimaced. "Ugh, my stomach," I called out in pain. "I gotta make a stop."

I made the right turn. The rest of the vehicles followed. The first portion of my impromptu scheme—get close to the tanning salon—complete, it was now time to execute the second phase. I knew that if I parked and got out, security and producers would be all over me before I could step foot in the salon. What if I slowed down to five miles per hour and jumped out while the vehicle was still moving? Then, Brad would have to jump into the driver's seat to stop the Escalade before it crashed. In the confusion, I figured I'd be able to run into the salon and take care of business. In my convoluted brain, that seemed like a perfectly reasonable strategy.

I executed the plan. With the car still in drive, I popped the door and leapt into the street. Landing on my feet, my momentum carried me forward into a sprint. I was off, a sight to behold—bright red Ed Hardy sweatpants, white guinea tee, rosary beads bouncing off my neck with a backwards baseball cap cocked *just* right. The Situation tore down the South Beach sidewalks while shocked tourists looked on. Behind me, I heard the security vehicles and cop car screech to a halt. I didn't bother looking back. I knew what I would see. The chase was on. Luckily, I had a nice head start.

I hit the front door of the tanning salon hard, bounding in and surprising anyone in the lobby. I knew the cops, security, and production team were all at a dead sprint headed toward me. I didn't have much time. My guy had no idea I'd be showing up right then, and he looked up from behind the front desk in shock as I shot through his tanning salon's front door. Instead of giving him the same imperceptible look I gave him every few days—our signal that I needed more pills—I screamed with urgency, "Give me the shit!"

With wide eyes, the owner of the tanning salon reached under the counter and tossed a fifty pack of Roxicet through the air. I scooped it off the floor and raced into the bathroom, locking it just as my pursuers entered the business. Within seconds, they were banging on the door, yelling for me to come out.

In one simultaneous, focused motion, I ripped open the baggy, popped four pills (rather than my normal six since I knew I was about to be interrogated and wanted to have my wits about me) in my mouth, stuffed the rest in my jockstrap, pulled out my phone, and dialed my attorney. When I finally opened the door and exited the bathroom, a mob of angry producers, security guards, and police officers were there to greet me.

"Mike, we know what you did," Brad said, almost like he was disappointed in me. I was intimately familiar with the tone. How they had discovered that the owner of this tanning salon was leaving prescription opiates under the towel in my tanning bed whenever I needed them was beyond me, but here we were.

It had been a pretty simple process while still an impressive feat to accomplish. The first time we filmed at this guy's tanning salon, I'd noticed his pinned pupils. I knew what that meant. It hadn't taken long for me to run through the opiate supply I'd smuggled into the house, and I was desperate for a connect in Miami. Despite being mic'd up and filmed twenty-four hours a day, I was able to silently communicate my wishes to the tanning salon owner, and the next thing I knew, I had a regular supply of pain pills delivered to me at the tanning salon. After I finished tanning, I would place his cash under the towel and go about my job with a fresh stash of pills hidden in my boxers. Having completed this same transaction dozens of times through most of the second season, I thought I was slick; ultimately, not slick enough.

I squeezed past everyone, holding out my phone. "I don't know what you're talking about. I had to use the bathroom. But feel free to talk to my lawyer if you want."

There really wasn't anything anyone could do, aside from stare at me with disgust. How had it come to this?

Like Hemingway once wrote about going bankrupt, the answer was "slowly, then all at once."

The insanity that had rapidly taken over my life began months before that South Beach chase, immediately after the *Jersey Shore* premiere. Overnight, I went from being broke and unknown with no fixed address to an international celebrity, unable to walk down the street without being mobbed. The stacks of cash I carried were so thick I couldn't even begin to count the money. Even by my standards, the number of beautiful women flocking to me increased to an unmanageable level, though I certainly tried.

Since the business side of entertainment wasn't my specialty, I knew early on that I needed to hire people I trusted to handle it all. The first thing I did as soon as we got a hint of how big this could be was to take the advice of Anthony Beltempo. He introduced me to Mike Petolino, whom I hired as my manager. I also enlisted my brother Marc, who had a master's degree in business from NYU and had already proven himself adept in the business world, to help set up an LLC.

We created MPS (Michael Paul Sorrentino) Entertainment and planned to run any new ventures through that entity. We had to start treating The Situation like a corporation, and these were the first steps. In the beginning, those measures were merely preemptive—just *in case* new business prospects came as a result of the show. Even though we had no way of knowing for sure, I felt like a wave of opportunity was headed my way.

Soon, those feelings were validated. As the episodes aired each week and the ratings skyrocketed, offers started pouring in. The Situation was suddenly big business.

Everyone wanted a piece. I began to feel like a passenger on an accelerating runaway train, hurdling along a trajectory I had no control over. All I could do was try to hold on for dear life. This is not to say I didn't enjoy it; enjoy it I certainly did—in hindsight, maybe a little too much. That initial onslaught was mind-blowing and at times overwhelming. The amount of money, sex, and fame thrust upon me so quickly was sometimes hard to fathom. Let me tell you, it *is* possible to have too much of a good thing.

Nightclub bookings came first. Mike Petolino, my new manager, had smartly brought a booking agency on board, and they quickly arranged a nightclub appearance tour. We rented a luxury bus and traveled up and down the East Coast, making at least one appearance a night, getting paid fifteen to twenty grand just to show up at a club and party. I brought my crew from home—my "day ones," the guys who always had my back—along to experience the good life and share this wild ride with me.

Touring the country and suddenly being treated like one of the Beatles instigated that dormant but familiar dance with my demons. The bad habits reintroduced themselves. It became easy to forget what had almost killed me the year before. After nearly twelve months of being clean of opiates, I began to dabble again at these parties where every substance was available and being offered to me. The pain of detoxing was easy to forget. Lines started to blur as I embraced the party and celebrity lifestyle; the next thing I knew, I was again regularly consuming Percocet, Valium, and Roxicet.

It was total hysteria at these parties. Exactly the way you would imagine it. They usually went something like this: We'd show up to the club and be greeted by a line of partiers wrapped around the building. Huge, raucous crowds, everyone dressed to the nines in mid-2000s regalia. I'd get out of the tour bus or limo, fresh to death, and a deafening round of cheers would erupt when the crowd saw me. As bass softly bumped from inside while spotlights and paparazzi flashes blinded us, we'd make our dash through the parking lot and to the entrance. Security would whisk us through a back door, usually to the owner's office. The first half of the appearance fee would have already been wired, so the owner or promoter would hand over a stack of cash for the remaining balance. Then, the festivities would commence. Use your imagination. Then, multiply it by a hundred.

I remember at one stop at a club in Canada, the owner was like, "I want you to meet these two girls, so-and-so and so-and-so." Then, with a self-important grin, he cleared out the rest of the room. Once he left, one of the girls turned to me. "This is my girlfriend. She's never been with a guy before!" My eyes widened with disbelief, and before I knew it, they were both on their knees. It happened that quickly. And that's just one fairly innocuous story. Something similar happened at nearly every single appearance. At a minimum, I had a threesome every night. Each stop introduced a new level of craziness.

After securing the bag from the owner, I'd go join the crowd in the club and do my thing. I partook in all the alcohol and party favors I wanted. After a few hours of posing for hundreds, if not thousands, of photos and emceeing the party, I'd go back on the tour bus or to the hotel where we'd continue the party.

My team would pick the hottest girls at each event. We'd ask if they wanted to party and if they were DTF. The answer was always yes and yes. We'd invite them back to the hotel, where adjoining rooms had been rented. I'd walk in, head to the master suite, and take out the drugs I wanted to do later. I knew clothes would be coming off soon and having them in my pockets did me no good. Cash, drugs, and other valuables would go in the safe because you didn't want random girls going through your stuff.

There would sometimes be as many as twenty-five girls in the room. I remember one time in the Midwest, there were just too many girls who wanted to get in. A large group made it into the room, but another was outside, banging on the door, trying to gain entrance. Hotel security was called, and we finally narrowed it down to ten women who could stay in the suite. I remember looking around at all these beautiful women, my mind just boggled at what my life had become.

A leader of the girls emerged. "Mike," she said, "you're not going to be able to handle all ten of us."

She was probably right. "What do you recommend?" I asked.

"Let's send one girl home and make three groups of three."

It sounded like a good plan to me. We kicked one girl out, leaving nine. They huddled to discuss which group of three would start the party and which group would be on deck to tap in. As they calculated, I started to realize what a tall task this was going to be. But hey, you'll never know if you don't try.

Then I started to hear the whispers of, "You don't tell my boyfriend, and I won't tell your boyfriend." I didn't like that. I put myself in the boyfriends' shoes and felt bad for them. But then my other head took over and I quickly dismissed that concern.

By now, the girls had worked out whatever they needed to work out, and everyone started to get naked. But as soon as we got down to it, one group of girls took out their phones and started to film. Uh-uh, that was a no-go. I jumped up and told them they had to leave. We were down to six. Still, I found the situation untenable and decided to kick out three more. Having narrowed it down to just the final three, the party kicked off, though new girls continued to arrive and bang on my door the rest of the night.

That's just the way it went back then. The VIP director of one hotel in Las Vegas told me that, other than George Clooney, he'd never seen anybody take back so many beautiful women before. They had to assign security just to help navigate the sea of girls trying to get into my room during the afterparty.

Whenever we got back to the hotel, I'd start by ordering room service—some chicken tenders and fries for the crew. Everyone would chill, have some drinks, and then the dancing and partying would start. Soon, all the clothes would be off.

I avoided the coke because one time early on during that tour, I experienced a bit of a situation during a stop in Jersey. Another set of ten drop-dead gorgeous girls, all of whom were soon naked and ready to sleep with me, had come back to my suite. It was going to be an orgy. But I'd done so much coke, I couldn't perform. I remember looking around the room, unable to believe this was my life. These girls were just happy being in my presence, ready to do whatever I wanted. All I could do was smile and marvel at the spectacle. I wasn't even upset the business wasn't going down; I was more in shock and disbelief that the opportunity had presented itself at all. And that it continued to every night.

After that experience, I always carefully strategized my drug intake. If I didn't, I'd never get to the finish line. Usually, after the fun with the girls was over, when they left or went to sleep, I took my Xanax and

Roxys and just chilled in bed, watching movies or something until ten or eleven in the morning. The squad would come in, pack everything up, and we'd head off to the next city to do it all over again.

Each morning, my boys would be suffering in pain and feeling like death while I was in good spirits and ready to play it back. The steady painkiller intake kept me numbly happy while eliminating the ill effects of no sleep and being hungover. Of course, this was early on in my opiate dependency before the negative effects began to take over.

Everywhere we went on that tour, I carried a Louis Vuitton bag like a security blanket. As I said, the promoters and club owners paid me half in cash at these appearances, and that bag was where I carried the money. I also kept my wallet in there, along with Chapstick, condoms, cigarettes, and anything else to keep the party going. It also doubled as my dispensary, filled with party favors: Xanax. Percocet. Valium. Roxicet. Adderall. Weed. Some coke. My tolerance was low back then, so 150 Percs and 150 Valiums got me through most of that first tour before season two. I do remember hoping we'd get some more gigs in the tri-state area whenever I got low since that's where the connects from my drug dealing days were located. I could always easily pick up a fifty pack or two back home.

It was, to say the least, not a healthy lifestyle. Terrible for me. Mentally, physically, and spiritually. I wasn't taking care of myself. Wasn't sleeping. I was self-medicating. Living minute by minute. Really, a textbook example of what not to do. But I'd be lying if I said I wasn't enjoying every minute of it. For a while, at least.

I felt fortunate to have so many people who were close to me by my side on that tour. It was satisfying to be able to take them along for the ride and to repay them for their loyalty. Guys like Johnny The Unit, one of my closest friends from childhood who let me crash with him for years and never charged me rent. Marc was there, mostly to try to keep me under control. A for effort, Marc. But seriously, it was a blessing to experience this madness and superstardom with the people who had always been there for me. They made it feel like home, even if I was usually too intoxicated to even know what state I was in.

The money was so crazy that at one stop, I don't remember where, Marc surprised me with a new Bentley. We got to the event, and it was just on display out front. I didn't even get to drive it. We took some photos in front of the car, then they had it shipped home because we had to get on the tour bus and hit the next city. That's the car that had the "Sitch" license plate.

It was just sex, drugs, and rock and roll, every day, all the time. Men wanted to be our best friends, and women wanted to sleep with us. It was crazy and started to mess with my head. I still couldn't believe this was my life. That old adage "be careful what you wish for" kicked in. It got to where I started to question what was so special about me. *Why are people obsessed with me? How and why is this happening?* It felt like a movie starring someone else playing me I guess.

As the nightclub tour wound down, I got a call from Dave, my attorney. Ever since that meeting in the city shortly after the show premiered when I shot down MTV's paltry offer for season two of *Jersey Shore*, my team had been working diligently to negotiate a fair deal for the next season. Dave informed me that the heavens had opened up. MTV had agreed to pay me what I deserved. It was a big deal. Multi-year. Obviously, we had to perform, but the numbers were staggering. A large signing bonus. A half-million-dollar rating bonus. The per episode fee started well above six figures and went up from there. Backend royalties that still pay handsomely to this day. In total, the contract was worth many millions. I felt like I had hit the jackpot.

The guidance was to not discuss my contract with anyone, but I later learned it mirrored Snooki's and Pauly's. I don't know what the others got; all I knew was my contract contained a stipulation stating no one on the show could make more than me.

Contract negotiations wrapped up just as the nightclub tour was winding down. In less than two weeks, shooting would begin in Miami for season two. I went home for a week to get packed and then headed down to Miami. The first thing I did was go Ferrari shopping with the crew as soon we arrived. (That was the "Sitch1" car.) Then, I went to Armani Exchange and bought out the store. Most importantly, I called up all my old drug dealing contacts and purchased five hundred Perc thirties. I figured that would be enough to get me through filming. As we know, that assumption was incorrect.

I put the pills in one of those ceramic bowls with the hammer-like crusher and ground them into powder. I then took three bottles of an herbal fat burner, emptied out the capsules, and refilled them with the Percocet powder. I knew security would be closely searching all our belongings when we arrived at the Miami house, and I needed to be prepared. The eye in the sky would still be watching, but to the producers, it would seem like I was just taking Xenadrine pills instead of what they really were: repackaged Perc sixties. Or at least I hoped they were. When you're filling your own capsules with opiates, it's pretty easy to get the dosage wrong.

And that's how I showed up to Miami for the second season—with what I foolishly assumed would be enough drugs to get me through filming. Of course, as so often occurred, I had severely underestimated my habit. With my supply dwindling, I was fortunate (or unfortunate) enough to make the aforementioned connect with the tanning salon owner. As we know, it was a relationship so valued that the prospect of losing it on one of the last days of filming resulted in that slow-speed car chase and subsequent foot race through the mean streets of South Beach.

It wouldn't be the last time MTV had to chase after me.

A taekwondo tournament in Miami in the early nineties. I would go on to earn a brown belt in the sport.

A collage of Lauren and I that she made when we were dating in college.

Brookdale Community College graduation in 2006 where I earned an associate degree in business management.

Lauren and I on vacation in Boca Raton with her family when we first started dating.

My sister, Melissa, and I at our brother Frank's wedding in Mexico.

One of the first photos Lauren and I took after we reconnected and started dating again.

Me, Pops, and my brother Marc right around the time the first episode of *Jersey Shore* was scheduled to premiere.

The four Sorrentino kids at the house we grew up in on Rowena Road in Manalapan, New Jersey.

Me and Mama Peaches in 2023.

A collage of me and my better half. Two of the photos were taken just after my release from prison. In both, Lauren was pregnant but would sadly miscarry.

JWoww and I before an awards show circa 2010.

Nicole and I in 2010.

My official casting photo for the
VH1 pilot that would become
MTV's *Jersey Shore*. With
clipboard girl at Harrah's in 2008.

The squad in Miami before the
official *Jersey Shore* reboot was
launched in 2018.

Me with my support network as a
guest of the government in Otisville.

Fans taking photos of me as I worked
in the iconic Shore Store in Seaside
Heights, New Jersey, while filming.

Just another night out with the squad. This time, backstage at an awards show with Mike Tyson and Snoop Dogg.

RSVP under a *Jersey Shore: Family Vacation* billboard in Los Angeles.

The squad out to dinner in LA after doing press.

Filming in upstate New York right after I was sentenced to eight months in prison. This was my bachelor party.

Having a situation with the girls from MTV's hit show *The Hills*.

At one of the thousands of appearances I did in the early 2010s.

Me pulling up to my tanning salon in my Lamborghini while filming *The Sorrentinos*.

The first two cars I purchased with my *Jersey Shore* millions. The Bentley license plate reads Sitch; the Ferrari's reads Sitch1.

One of the best days of my life—when my daughter Mia Bella was born.

Precious Situations. My beautiful children, Romeo Reign and Mia Bella Sorrentino.

Reading my own press about my work at rehab facilities. After a few years of sobriety, the narrative was changing.

Keeping the tradition going: our first vacation in Boca with our growing family.

Signing my plea agreement with the government that I thought would prevent me from going to prison. I was wrong.

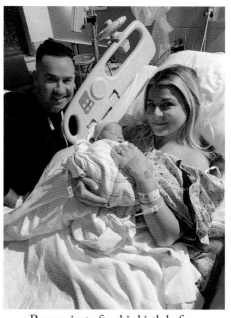

Romeo just after his birth before we found out about his fever.

Me and Romeo swimming at our home in Holmdel, New Jersey, in 2023.

Living my best sober dad life.

CHAPTER 13

THE GRIP GETS TIGHTER

By the time that second season wrapped, my brain was fried from the whirlwind of drugs, hookups, and round-the-clock filming. I was still attempting to adjust to this relatively new and overwhelming fame, and my (mis)management of these nuclear life changes while locked in the grip of active addiction meant I was barely holding on. But before we could leave Miami, production needed to film the final interviews, a process that could be brutal.

Final interviews occur at the end of every season and mean up to six hours with producers and cameras as they grill you about everything and anything that took place that season. It was up to each of us to decide if and how we answered. This was our chance to put our truth out there, and if our responses were consistent with reality and the direction the producers wanted to move the story in, they would air them.

On this particular day, I took my seat and prepared for the same type of softball questions they always asked: "What do you think about Ronnie and Sam's relationship?" "What did you think about the content of 'the note'?" "Describe the boys' entry to the club that night." Basic questions designed to add color to the storylines. But on this day, they dropped a bomb on me.

"Do you have a drug problem?"

My jaw dropped. I couldn't believe this producer had just asked me that. The accuracy of the inquiry seemed irrelevant and, in fact, never entered my consideration. Was it true? Of course! Did I think they should ask me that? At the time, absolutely not! The question seemed totally and completely out of bounds to me. Where was this coming from? I was furious. In my hazy, high brain, those were fighting words. What kind of show was this? This wasn't what I signed up for! *This show is about young people partying, and they're trying to throw that in my face?*

I used the offensive question as an opportunity to immediately bounce from the interview and once again wreak havoc. Standing, I started pulling off my mic. "Go fuck yourself," I growled at the producer, throwing the mic at him and walking out of the interview.

I was in denial about my addiction, so deep in it that I couldn't see my nose in front of my face. The way I looked at it, they never asked any of us about drug or alcohol use. I didn't think that storyline should be part of the show.

Gradually, I walked through the house, working myself up, growing more incensed with each passing second. *How dare they! I can't believe these people are trying to take this in that direction! Are they asking other people about their heavy drinking? Their drug use? They're trying to take me down!* Eventually, I'd hyped myself up so much that I found my feet carrying me toward the exit at the back of the house.

Several producers followed close behind, their addresses urgent while remaining gently conservative, afraid that if they pushed too hard, I'd be gone, or if they didn't push hard enough, the same result would occur. Little did they know the outcome was predetermined. This was a lose-lose for them. They got closer and closer, calling out, pleading, "Mike, come on, stop! I'm sorry. We won't use that!"

By this point, I had worked myself into such a rage that I bolted past security and out the door. The guards stationed outside were there to keep random people out of the house. The star of the show just speed-walked past them and they didn't know whether to stop me or not. I didn't give them a chance to decide. Suddenly, it was déjà vu all over again. I booked it past everyone, just like I had ten days prior, running down the streets of South Beach with a fleet of producers and security trying to keep up.

Just like before, The Situation, shining like a neon sign in full guido uniform (this time, the Ed Hardy pants were a bright sky blue), sprinted from production while random people on the street watched and screamed my name.

Ahead, I saw an idling taxi. I dove into the back seat in a graceful swan dive like freaking Superman, shouting, "go, go, go!" reminiscent of an eighties cop movie. The driver hit it, and I peeked over the headrest in time to witness the MTV crew getting smaller and smaller through the back window. I breathed a sigh of relief and smiled. Escape complete. I was free, at least for a little while. Which was all I wanted.

I had the cabbie pull over at the next light. I jumped out, ran into a store, and asked if I could use their phone. It was like your one call from jail—make it count. I wracked my brain, thinking of anyone in Miami who could give me the help I was looking for. The answer was obvious: The Unit. He was in town. I knew I could always count on The Unit.

Back at his apartment, the focus turned to getting drugs. Unit wasn't a drug dealer, but he knew people I could score with. While he worked on that, I fielded calls from everyone from my brother to the president of MTV. I told the head of the network how disrespected I felt. Acting insulted, I asked him, "What kind of show is this, trying to make me look like a drug addict?"

The irony was, of course, that I *was* a raging drug addict, and the question had been completely in bounds. But at the time, I didn't want to hear it. The head honcho apologized to me, claiming it was a miscommunication, and promised they wouldn't bring that up again or use any of the footage. He agreed to personally ensure any suspicion of drug addiction would not be part of the storyline. He also made it very clear they needed me back on set immediately.

"Sure," I told him. "I just need a few hours to cool off first. Then, I'll go back." Of course, it was all bullshit. I was just procrastinating. An excuse to buy me time for the only thing I was concerned about: getting more pills. Because, you see, this whole thing wasn't about being offended by the producer's question. I couldn't have cared less about the question. The truth was I was getting low on pills and needed a diversion to reup. I'd seen an opportunity and seized it without thought. That's really what all the manufactured outrage was about: escaping for a few hours so I could feel like a free man and get high without having to sneak around in front of my castmates and production. Sadly, that's what freedom meant to me during that time.

The Unit was able to touch base with one of my contacts down there so I could cop a fifty pack of Perc thirties. After popping a few, I was good as new, quickly demonstrating my uncanny ability to forget everything that had just transpired. Happy, high, and with a pocket full of opiates, I headed back to the house like nothing had happened. After the scene I'd just made, I knew there was no way they were going to search me.

It became clear to everyone but me that my addiction had reappeared with a vengeance, clenching me in a ferocious hold I wasn't even aware of at the time. My opiate consumption grew into an unmanageable habit that season. I was high all the time, taking upwards of twenty pills a day. Trying to hide it from my employer, I would sneak them in the bathroom every couple of hours. I was barely holding on while my behavior was, to say the least, out of control.

There had been a devil's threesome in Miami with Vinny and a girl we brought home from the club that MTV never aired. I remember thinking in the middle of it, *Damn, there's a whole production crew in the control room watching this*. I didn't care. I grabbed a pillow and held it over my butt, but unable to focus on the task at hand, I eventually gave up and dropped it. I'm sure the control room got a good show. No one ever mentioned it.

Another scene they didn't air that season in Miami occurred on one of the last days of production, just before those final interviews. Incredibly high and ecstatic we had wrapped our second season, I channeled my inner rock star and began to destroy the house like I was Pete Townshend after a The Who concert. Smiling the entire time, I threw all the furniture outside onto that green patio. SallyAnn Salsano, the boss bitch who owned the whole damn show and ran it with an iron fist, someone who always kept us in line and whom we had the utmost respect for, came sprinting out of the production room screaming at me, not for the first time. I turned to her and kind of shrugged, still smiling. I was like, *Isn't this what you want?* To me, it was like *Gladiator*: "Are you not entertained?" I didn't think there was anything wrong with my behavior, even when I was destroying property. I looked at it like the last day of school when anything goes.

The truth was my behavior was becoming more and more erratic, and I grew more and more uncontrollable. Looking back now, I realize I had turned into a madman. My designation as public enemy number one on *Jersey Shore* was a well-earned and fair one.

My behavior affected everyone around me. The rest of the cast walked on eggshells. Those once-strong relations began to decay due to my outlandish and toxic actions. These people whom I was sharing such an amazing experience with no longer wanted to be in my company. And I can't blame them. I was a loose cannon—no one knew who I would turn on next.

The first season down the shore had been fun. Innocent. Just young, good-looking guidos partying. But it wasn't like that anymore. Miami had been different. Everything was bigger, more amplified, and my conduct and drug use was putting it all at risk. As good of a heart as I thought I had, my actions were disturbing. Hence why my castmates no longer wanted to have anything to do with me off camera. The dynamic trio of MVP—Mike, Vinny, and Pauly, three guys who had become like brothers while entertaining millions—fractured. Vinny and Pauly began to rightfully second-guess our friendship after my behavior in Miami. A big part of the show had been built on those relationships, and that storyline went missing.

I was in such a drug-induced fog, I didn't notice any of it happening. It would take years to gain the clarity and self-awareness required to see the damage I'd done. I just kept being me, or at least who I was at thet time: a wild, polarizing personality that the people I was closest with didn't want to be around.

Production, crew, and castmates didn't have hard evidence of my drug abuse, nor did they understand the full extent of it, but they had a pretty good idea what was going on. It couldn't have been hard for the people I spent 24/7 with to put the pieces together. They saw the brazen behavior. My constantly pinned pupils. The aggressive excitement to get to the tanning salon. Combine those things with the sudden escapes and disappearing acts, and the writing was on the wall. Still, for the most part, my drug problem went unmentioned until that final interview. I mean, we're all Italian, and in our culture, you don't usually talk about these things in the open. Besides, what were they going to do? I didn't listen to anyone.

But by the end of that season, Jenni, being someone never afraid to speak her mind, had had enough of my antics and finally confronted me on air. MTV depicted our fight in such a way that the audience couldn't tell what we were fighting about, but the truth is it was about my addiction and drug use. I don't even think she ever specifically said "drug addict," as the whole subject was a gray area. Obviously, telling on someone else was taboo, but I was hurting myself and the show, so she felt like she had a right to say something.

In hindsight, of course she did, but back then, you can guess what my reaction was. Jenni calling me out came from a place of concern, but I didn't want to hear it. I wasn't ready to provide full disclosure to the world about just how deep my addiction ran. I wasn't ready to admit that my demons were winning this battle.

And while everyone else was presumably able to put two and two together, they didn't have any proof. But Jenni did. Previously, during some rigorous press and promo appearances, I gave myself away by offering her an eighty-milligram Oxy after a particularly grueling and stressful day. Jenni declined, but from then on, she knew what I was doing. And that's why she felt justified in bringing it up. I just wasn't ready to listen.

After filming in Miami wrapped, we all went back to our respective lives. Those splintering relationships with my castmates became nonexistent. I had no interactions with any of them off-season. But again, I was in such high demand and so out of my mind that I didn't notice or care. I was in survival mode.

CHAPTER 14

A CELEB TO CELEBRITIES

Instead of life slowing down with the conclusion of filming the second season of *Jersey Shore*, it sped up to what felt like warp speed. Life during those years was pretty fuzzy. My drug-addled mind remained in a perpetual haze, and a lot got thrown at me in a short period of time. I did my best, but there's a lot I didn't handle correctly.

GQ named me their "Sensation of the Year" in 2010, which was an immense honor, but of all the people who made their list, I was the only one who didn't get a cover. There was this perception that reality stars weren't real stars, which I obviously disagreed with. Hey, *GQ*, you still owe me that cover…

I was also approached about doing that Calvin Klein underwear campaign, something that was a long-time dream of mine. Foolishly, my team declined, thinking I should get more money than what they were offering. I believe Calvin Klein offered $50k, and my team countered with half a million dollars. Needless to say, negotiations didn't go much farther after that. What we didn't realize was that you don't do a Calvin Klein ad for the money; you do it for the prestige. But I thought I was such a superstar that the rules didn't apply to me. Of course, I now wish I had taken that opportunity.

Ego and ignorance also lost me an endorsement deal with Lamborghini. A dealership in Florida proposed making a special "Situation" Lambo for me. Everything is so blurry from that time period that I can't be positive on the exact details, but I'm pretty sure the reason my team turned that one down was because they only offered to let me keep one Lamborghini. We thought I should get two. I couldn't say for sure though—I was probably on a plane flying to an appearance after taking a handful of Percocets when my team raised the proposal. Either way, there were so many offers and so few occasions when I was thinking clearly that I made a lot of bad decisions.

I was burnt out and neglecting my health, never taking the time for any self-care or rest. Weeks after filming season two in Miami, I headed out to LA to train for and film *Dancing with the Stars*. I didn't know anyone out there, so I devised a way for a dealer I grew up with to FedEx me pills from Jersey. He'd remove the guts of a pen, fit twenty-five Roxys in it, then close the pen and stick it in an overnight FedEx package with a couple pads of paper so it would look like someone was mailing school supplies. He'd send me ten pens at a time for regular shipments of 250 pills. The scheme worked perfectly. So well, in fact, that once, when the delivery driver was late, I had the audacity to call the FedEx customer service line and question them as to why my package of drugs wasn't on time.

I needed those pills for DWTS. That was one of the hardest shows I've ever done. I practiced eight hours a day, popping six Perc thirties every few hours. I remember right before a live show, Rick Fox and David Hasselhoff came up to me backstage. Everyone else was petrified about performing, taking shots and doing anything they could to calm their nerves. Not me.

"Man, you are stone cold," they said with admiration in their eyes. "You must have ice in your veins. You don't look nervous at all."

I shrugged and smiled. Yeah, because I was high as fuck. I barely knew where I was. Who knows how I responded, but I didn't tell them my secret.

I made it through four rounds of DWTS. The night we were eliminated, I ran out of pills. The thing to do after being eliminated from DWTS was rush over to Jimmy Kimmel and do his show. "Uh-uh, no way," I told everyone at the network. "I'm not going on shit unless I get some painkillers."

At some point during the course of the show, I might have slightly tweaked my neck or back, so I started milking that, telling the ABC doctor he needed to prescribe me some Oxy. He only wanted to give me some low-level pain medication, but I insisted on something stronger, claiming I was in severe pain. It wasn't true, of course, but what was he going to say? Eventually, he gave me what I wanted, and I made my team run out to fill the script before I would do the show.

I went on Kimmel high as hell, but that was alright. I was used to it. I was a pro by this point. I'd gone on Jimmy Fallon, Jay Leno, and pretty much every other talk show plenty of times, usually stoned on painkillers. I knew the drill. Though maybe my habit was a little more obvious than I thought. A couple of times, Jay pulled me aside after appearances on *The Tonight Show*. I could see the concern in his face. He'd witnessed it before and wanted to straighten me out.

"You've got to make better decisions," Jay Leno told me on more than one occasion. He was a super nice guy, and I felt he was looking out for me. "You're never going to last in this business going the way you are." He was right, of course, though again, it would be some time before I was ready to listen.

Whoopi Goldberg was another one who spotted the tell-tale signs of my addiction and tried to call attention to my actions. Many times, she graciously reached out to warn me that I was moving too fast. She had a very loving and caring manner about her that I will never forget.

A meaningful conversation I had with Robert Downey, Jr., backstage on *The Today Show* around this time also left an impact on me. As someone who had gone through the same addiction issues I was grappling with at the time, he recognized the signs: glasses tipped low, pupils pinpointed, my energy douchebag on blast. Ours was a quick run-in, but the pleasantries quickly turned into a serious conversation. I remember he showed concern for my condition and implored me to be careful.

But I thought I was just having fun, enjoying this immense gift of fame and fortune that had been bestowed upon me. The way I looked at it, I wasn't doing anything wrong. I wasn't hurting anyone. But in reality, I wasn't making the good decisions required to nurture those blessings.

The next debacle was the Trump roast. Donald Trump graciously and generously flew me out to New York on his private jet and put me up in one of the best suites in the Trump Tower. Comedy Central paid me six figures to participate in his roast. It was a fun experience, even if it turned out to be a disaster.

I went into the show having never read the script. The writers handed it to me about an hour before the roast, and I never so much as looked at it, let alone read it or practiced my delivery. I was only concerned with how I looked—making sure my outfit and hair were on point. I didn't know the jokes until I tried to read them off the teleprompter. Comedy isn't easy, and this first attempt went about as badly as it possibly could. My timing and tone were completely off, and if you've seen the cringe-worthy clips, you know how horribly I bombed.

Still, I took it as victory. Yes, it was the most awkward thing ever. Yes, I was high as giraffe balls. No, I didn't care about getting booed, mostly due to being so high. And yes, it was one of the most-watched roasts Comedy Central ever aired.

It was funny. After the show, I received no boos or taunts from the people in the audience. No cold shoulders. Quite the opposite, in fact. Per usual, all the other celebs were enthralled with me. They crowded around me, wanting to talk and take pictures, seemingly completely forgetting what had just transpired on stage.

Mr. Trump was very nice about the whole thing. He told me I handled myself well. Jeff Ross had come up on stage and tried to help me out, which was cool. Snoop Dogg, John Legend, and Chrissy Teigen, whose viral "cringe face" meme emanated from that roast, told me they were huge fans.

That's the way it was back then. I was like a celebrity to celebrities. Actors get to play "cool" on TV. I did it in real life, and other celebs were always in disbelief that I was a real person when we met.

After the roast, I entertained everyone for a while, laughing it up and being my charming self, but I couldn't help but feel lonely in this sea of celebrities. I made my exit and headed back to my room.

Earlier that day, I had sprinted through the front doors of Trump Tower as TMZ chased behind, snapping a million pictures and shouting questions. I bumped into Ben Stiller in the lobby, and he stared at me, kind of in shock.

"Damn, man, does that ever get exhausting?" he asked.

I shrugged and probably just hit him with my well-known smirk. "Dunno. It happens all the time. I barely even notice anymore."

That's the way it was. A few months earlier, Mike Tyson and I were presenting at the same awards show. At one point, he leaned over and whispered in my ear, "Keep slaying these hoes." Another time, before the Billboard Music Awards, after my normal sprint through the paparazzi gauntlet, I reached my hotel lobby, exhausted and a little dope sick, shades on and hat pulled low. Short-term goals included getting to my room, showering, and getting my fix. After those boxes were checked, I knew everything would be peaches.

As I rode up the escalator, in a rush to start the process, I looked over and noticed someone else trying to roll in incognito. It dawned on me that it was Drake, also in sunglasses with hat pulled low, looking equally depleted. We realized at the same time we were both doing the same thing—international stars trying our hardest to escape to our rooms without being noticed. Neither of us could help laughing, and when we reached the top of the escalator, we dapped each other up and took a photo together before heading off to our respective rooms.

Another interaction during that time that's worth mentioning—if only because it was recently dug up again by Steve-O on his wildly successful podcast, and I'd like to set the record straight—is when I bumped into the *Jackass* crew on the VMA red carpet back in 2010. As they tell it, I "cool guy'd" them, claiming I brushed them off when they tried to talk with me.

Being a HUGE *Jackass* fan, I *never* would have knowingly done that! But I had just popped 180 milligrams of Percocet in the limo before walking down the red carpet and was in my own little world while about a thousand people screamed my name and flashbulbs went off in my face. I remember looking to my left and seeing the *Jackass* crew getting interviewed next to me with Rick Ross on my right. I was a huge fan of both but so fucked up that I was forced to perch my sunglasses on the bridge of my nose to hide the fact that I couldn't see straight. I assure you, Steve-O, Wee Man, Johnny Knoxville, Preston, et al—I did not try to snub you guys and still love you!

Back in my Trump Tower suite after the roast, I felt sort of confused. I had just failed miserably in front of a live audience of superstars and a TV audience of millions. I'd been booed off the stage and made fun of mercilessly. But an hour later, everyone loved me again. They all wanted to be around The Situation, even after I bombed. It should have been embarrassing, but it wasn't. No one treated me as if it were. It was such a mindfuck. I felt tired. Sad. Empty and lonely.

I started to think back to when I'd last been happy. Truly happy. Before the money, fame, and adoration. It occurred to me it had been when I possessed nothing materialistic. Just the love of a good woman.

I lay on the bed, staring at the ceiling, reminiscing. My thoughts kept going back to Lauren. My one true love. The One. I knew she had moved on with her life. I'd heard whispers she had a serious boyfriend and was probably getting engaged soon. That's what I wanted for myself, but I was stuck in this other life with no escape.

I decided to call her right then and there. We hadn't talked in a while, really since the craziness of the show had started a year and a half earlier. I was dying to hear her voice.

So I called my college sweetheart with no expectation other than hoping she would answer. She did, and I tried to convince her to end her relationship and come back to me. She said no, she couldn't do that, but hearing the pain in my voice, she agreed to stay on the phone with me. To be there for me and talk me off the ledge as a friend. That meant a lot. If nothing else, I could tell she still cared. We hung up, and this crazy life went on.

The next time I called Lauren, a month or so later, the number was no longer in service. I later discovered that when she'd told her boyfriend I had called, he made her change her number. I wondered if that was the end of us.

Over the next couple of years, every time I was back in Jersey, I'd drive by her house like some crazy stalker, hoping to bump into her or her parents. I'd rev my Ferrari's or Lamborghini's engine as I sped down her street in Holmdel, blasting Drake's "Marvin's Room," making as much noise as possible in the hopes she'd look out a window and see it was me. You know, get a glimpse of the rich, famous guy she used to date. The one who got away. It was pitiful, but the story in that song was perfect. Exactly what I was trying to do—court and get back my lost love.

I had everything I thought I ever wanted but not what I really needed. It would be like that for a while.

Things would get worse before they got better.

CHAPTER 15

SITUATION, INC.

If you're tiring of the accounts of how fast and crazy my life was accelerating during this time, believe me, living it was exponentially more exhausting.

But the reality is everything—my drug addiction, the incoming money, and the demand for The Situation—continued to escalate at an astounding pace. The only thing exceeding my insatiable opiate appetite was my ego. Yes, I became fully drunk on The Situation Kool-Aid. I did what I wanted, when I wanted, with whom I wanted. No one told me "no."

The incoming money was crazy, though I never really knew how much it all amounted to. Network checks of $700,000 landed every few episodes. The high-paying endorsements and gigs kept coming: A protein-infused vodka. GTL laundry bags. The Situation line of tuxedos and other clothing. There was some juvenile GTL book I put no effort into, especially compared to the dedication I now understand goes into writing a great book. There was also a comic book loosely based on my escapades. Bobbleheads. Then, of course, royalties on everything *Jersey Shore* related. Topps even did a *Jersey Shore* baseball card. I had a tanning salon sponsorship and a Situation spray tan. A twenty-five-dollar Situation lollipop made by Sugar Factory. We released a song with Fatman Scoop, a workout video, and a line of rosary beads. So many tchotchkes, trinkets, and other crap that I could barely keep track of it all. But I knew it paid well.

It wasn't just the insane amounts of money. Everyone wanted to take their piece of me. And for the most part, I loved it. I got off on it.

Once, I was rushing through the airport to find The Rock holding up his gate to have a word with me after he heard I was in his terminal. He was so excited to meet me. The Rock! "You know, Situation," he boomed in that famous voice as he wrapped me in a bear hug, "America loves you. You branded yourself, and no one taught you how to do it. I'm impressed, my man."

I was blown away. The Rock was one of my idols. He had no way of knowing it, but The Situation character was modeled after him. I had emulated his wrestling persona when developing my over-the-top, exaggerated on-screen character, and now he was seeking me out to shake my hand. Yet another surreal moment on a long and growing list.

There was the time I boarded my flight either super high or super tired (probably a combo of both) and immediately fell asleep upon taking my window seat in first class. Next thing I knew, I woke to the flight attendant laughing to someone, "I think you have a situation." I squinted through blurry vision to make out a bald-headed guy standing over me. Evidently, I was in his seat, though his big grin suggested he didn't mind. I realized it was Jason Statham, another actor I'm a huge fan of. He laughed and told me to keep the seat, and he took the aisle. I later heard him tell that story on a late-night talk show.

Another funny incident occurred in LA at what I believe was an MTV-organized dinner for some of their biggest stars. At the time, *The Hills* was one of the network's top-rated shows. Those girls were the OG reality stars, but they couldn't wait to get a piece of The Situation. The second we walked in the door, they ravaged me. I mean, ripped my clothes off. Hands rubbing all over my abs and, ahem, maybe some other places too... I had no choice in the matter, not that I disapproved.

The sad part is the only reason I remember that night is because I have a photo of Kristin Cavallari on her knees, kissing my abs while lifting my shirt up. (Take that, Jay Cutler. You may have beaten me in cornhole, but I, uh, never mind...)

I was so intoxicated for so many years, I wonder how many crazy interactions like that simply never registered in my brain and are now lost to history. Too many.

Another time, Snooki, Pauly, and I were summoned to LA for some press requests. One of our appearances was on some internet show Ashton Kutcher was doing live on the web. During that interview, he told us about an emerging social media platform called Twitter. He recommended we sign up for it, and then and there, live on his show, he created Twitter handles for the three of us. At first, he tried @TheSituation for me, but I believe that username was taken. So he typed in @itsTheSituation, which was available. My following quickly skyrocketed to well over a million people, and that's still the handle I use today.

When my team and I weren't working and traveling the world, our favorite place to party was South Beach. I'd ship a few Ferraris and Lambos down to Frank's condo on Collins Avenue, and I'd pay for the whole crew to go down there for sometimes months at a time. That was our chance to enjoy the fruits of our labor. Marc wouldn't stay as long as I did, and the real party would begin once he went back to Jersey.

We enjoyed the sun, sand, and nightclubs. LIV was our favorite, and the owner, Dave Grutman, always escorted us to a private VIP booth and made sure we were well taken care of. We tore it up down there, enjoying every second as we lived life by the seat of our pants. A standard night could mean hanging with Lil Wayne or taking shots with Tiësto. Leave the club in a car service and bring back as many girls as could fit in the limos. Get food from Big Pink and then do what consenting adults do. At the time, I was living like a king, though a foolish one. I hadn't yet contemplated that pride cometh before the fall. It was a fast lifestyle, and my mentality was *you only live once*. Of course, at the rate I was going, it wasn't going to be for a long time.

If this lifestyle sounds appealing, it's because you've never experienced it. I may have been living a life that many dream of, but it was hard to turn the decadence off. Yes, there were a lot of great parts about being The Situation back then, but also some not-so-great ones. For all the amazing experiences, it could be exhausting living like that in the throes of active addiction. Suffering in silence while trying to hide my habit from the world was not easy. That was the reason for the trademark sunglasses I wore everywhere I went (oh yeah, I had a sunglasses line as well). People assume they were just part of my persona, which is partially true. But they also hid my always tiny pupils, constricted from opiate use.

On top of being completely dependent on these pills, it was lonely residing on this summit of reality TV stardom. I had no relationships with my castmates. I had trouble maintaining normal relationships because it felt like everyone wanted something from me. And my internal team was in shambles with constant in-fighting between my brother Marc and my manager Mike Petolino. Their conflicting personalities were another unnecessary and taxing stressor. Being constantly high meant I could avoid most negative emotions, but they remained ever present, lurking under the surface, just waiting to be released.

Finally, the tension between Marc and Mike got so bad that I had to make a decision. My brother thought we could handle the tidal wave of incoming business by ourselves. While Mike was doing a good job for me, an argument could be made that there were too many cooks in the kitchen. Now, the flip side of that coin is that checks and balances are a good thing for any business. You need people with different points of view. But at the end of the day, I just wanted peace, and these two clashed over everything.

I finally decided to let Mike, my first manager, go. All business would now be conducted in house by family. Marc, my other brother Frank, my sister Melissa, my mom, even my best friend, Pete, all worked for me. I figured the move would save me money as well as foster a sense of peace in the Situation camp.

I was wrong.

Like with most of my choices back then, I wasn't thinking clearly or making educated decisions. Instead of saving me money, firing Mike ended up costing me $250,000 when he (rightfully) sued me for terminating his contract early. I never consulted Dave, my attorney, before firing Mike. Unfortunately, it was common for me to make important, life-altering decisions on an intoxicated whim, a trait that would cost me for years.

But at the time, I wasn't concerned. I didn't have the mental bandwidth to worry about issues like finances and lawsuits. Season three of *Jersey Shore* was about to start shooting, and I needed to make sure I had enough narcotics to get me through filming. The MTV brass, tired of chasing after me, had put a clause in my contract that they could now go after my money if I took off like I had in season two. The situation just got real.

It was imperative I didn't run out of drugs mid-filming again. Once more, I purchased and crushed up five hundred pills to smuggle into the shore house, relying on the old diet pill switcheroo. For the most part, it worked. Miraculously, I had judged correctly and didn't need to concoct any escapes to reup. Season three is a little fuzzy because, well, I consumed five hundred pills during it, but it seemed to go pretty smoothly.

After filming wrapped, it was more of the same. I did another night-club tour while the train continued speeding down the track. I couldn't tell that it was starting to lose control.

I was worn down. I wondered when the ride was going to slow and let me off. I needed a break but couldn't get it. There were too many things pulling me in too many different directions. If only I had recognized that it was my habit doing this to me. If I had been healthy and clean, I would have easily been able to handle such a busy schedule. But I was in a different world, and the schedule I was keeping was taking its toll.

CHAPTER 16

HITTING A WALL

Season four was to shoot in Italy. Right off the bat, I knew that location would prove to be more difficult to smuggle pills into. Ever since receiving notice filming would occur there, the rest of the cast had been excited about spending time in the mother country. Not me. My fixation remained on how I was going to get enough pills through customs to keep me high the entire time we were in Italy.

I settled on a new caper. I could fit 125 Roxicets into an Altoid tin. I filled four tins. Then, I removed the cushions from the inside of a pair of shoes—red and black Filas, I remember, my favorite shoes that season—and cut out enough room in the heel to place two Altoids tins in each shoe. I then replaced the insole and packed the kicks in a large suitcase with twenty other pairs. My thought process was that with all those shoes, airport security wouldn't catch the five hundred opiate pills I was smuggling into a foreign country.

And I was right. The suitcase made it through immigration, no problem. Next, my concern turned to the show's security. In my experience, they were significantly more diligent than TSA. It's been well-documented that MTV was onto my habits and went to great pains to thwart my shenanigans and, as a result, subjected me to significant levels of scrutiny and a thorough examination of my belongings to ensure this exact thing was not occurring.

But I had a plan for that too. When security got to my shoe suitcase during their search, they were already exhausted from going through my other eight bags with a fine-tooth comb. I called out, "Oh wow, the Filas will go perfect with this outfit! I'm going to wear them now." I snatched the shoes and put them on my feet, thus taking the offending footwear out of the equation. After beelining it to the bathroom, I removed the insole, retrieved my treasure chest, popped six pills, and was good as new. If you notice, I rocked those black and red Filas more than any other shoes that season for obvious strategic reasons.

The Italy season wasn't my best season. In fact, it was my worst. My continued toxic behavior further fatigued my castmates. By this point, these relationships were hanging on by a thread. They didn't want to be around me. Again, I don't blame them for not liking me. I wasn't nice. I was very confrontational. I wasn't pleasant to be around. I would argue with anyone willing to engage, and I always went straight for the throat. I had fallen into the role of the "bad guy," and my mindset switched to, *okay, if I'm the bad guy, then I'm going to be the BAD GUY.* To me, it was like another scene in *Scarface*: "Say good night to the bad guy!" I embraced the role.

But my castmates had no idea what I was dealing with. Not really. They were unaware of the extent of my addiction, if they even knew about it at all. They certainly couldn't have understood the dark and terrible place I'd fallen into by this point. I worked hard to hide it, but the manner in which I was living my life left me so tired and empty that I couldn't catch my breath. This wasn't a sustainable way to live but rather a recipe to die young. My outlandish proclivities served as a silent cry for help while everything slowly collapsed around me.

Things went from bad to worse. As I tended to do, I had underestimated my habit and ran out of pills with a week or so left in the Italy season.

The whole time, I'd been telling myself to slow down. In my head, I said I'd take less. I promised myself that instead of taking six pills, next time I'd take two. Or four. Instead, I'd take seven, eight. I kept making and breaking deals with myself. *If I take pills now, I won't take any again until tomorrow.* Eight hours later, I would swallow another handful, promising myself I would make up for it by just taking two in the morning so I wouldn't feel sick. You can guess how that went. I broke every single bargain I made until the inevitable happened: I was out of drugs in a strange country where I had no idea how or where to get more. I was furious at myself for getting into this situation. I had the resources.

Why hadn't I packed more pills? I'd known that I was running low, but instead of taking less, I'd taken more. This was a hell of my own making.

Every time we walked down the street and I saw the pharmacy signs, I'd fantasize about filling a prescription so I wouldn't go through withdrawals on camera in front of millions. But I didn't know their policies or what painkillers they used in Italy. I was stuck and feeling worse by the day. I tried to mask the inevitable dope sickness with copious amounts of alcohol since that was not only easy to get but socially acceptable and encouraged. To an extent, it worked, but I was a ticking timebomb. I said before that it felt like I was a passenger in this speeding car that was my life; now, it was more like I had been duct taped and thrown in the trunk. Any sense of control over my own life was long gone.

By the time I hit day three of my involuntary detox in Italy, I was crawling the walls. I couldn't sleep. No longer high for the first time in more than a year, I fruitlessly ducked for cover as all my buried emotions and fears came shooting up in a sea of depression, anxiety, and anger.

I was in a horrible mental space when Ronnie decided it was time to address his issues with me. Tensions between the two of us had been building each season, and now, after a night of hard drinking, he probably saw what poor shape I was in and decided to confront me. To catch me in a vulnerable state. Sick and depressed, I snapped. I hit a wall, literally and figuratively.

If you don't know what I mean, go back and watch that fight scene. All the angst I was enduring boiled up, and for some reason, I decided to launch myself at the wall headfirst. That's right—to show Ronnie how ready I was to throw down, I headbutted a wall. A wall that, like in the States, I was expecting to be sheetrock. No, no, no, not in Italy. Unbeknownst to me, this was some ten-thousand-year-old cement wall from the fucking Romans or some shit. Like, Caeser may have headbutted this thing back in the day when he got in a fight with his roommate. As soon as The Situation's forehead impacted that cement, I tumbled to the floor like a sack of potatoes. You know how in the cartoons the characters see stars after a head injury? Yeah, that was me.

Jenni leaned over my prone body on the floor. She thought I was dead. All I could think was, *Damn, America is never going to forgive me for this. I gotta get up and fight this kid.*

So I did. The adrenaline was in overdrive. I blinked a few times and shook off the headache splitting my cranium, partially from withdrawals, partially from the wall, and we got it on.

The fight wasn't much. More like a wrestling match. From the viewpoint of the camera, it may have looked like Ronnie got the better of me, but no punches were landed, just a few wild swipes. A little tousle that bruised my ego more than anything.

My neck, however, was worse off from the wall. They called an ambulance, and I was taken to the hospital. The diagnosis was a concussion and sprained neck, hence the famous neck brace I had to wear for the rest of the season.

Pauly went to the hospital, and I remember him being like, "Mike, it's Paul. Can you hear me?" It was a surreal moment—lying in a hospital bed in Italy, eyes closed, neck in a brace, head ringing. My skin was also crawling, stomach cramping, and I was breaking out in cold sweats from withdrawals. I was in rough shape.

The only good thing about the headbutt was that, inadvertently, it got me what I wanted. They prescribed me painkillers despite MTV telling the doctors not to give me anything. But it was only some weak codeine that barely took the edge off.

To say I was miserable would be a gross understatement. Adding another layer to the depth of my pain, my father and I had a falling out while I was shooting in Italy. He's old school and didn't agree with how I made a living. It would take years of not speaking before we finally reconnected after realizing life was finite. We now talk regularly, and I'm grateful he's back in my life.

My emotions were in the basement. I called my sister, distraught and exhausted, and told her I thought this was going to be my last season of *Jersey Shore*. I couldn't do it any longer. I was sick and tired of being sick and tired. Filming was set to conclude in the next couple of days, and

I couldn't wait to get home and get a break. I needed to go directly to either my drug dealer or to rehab. I hadn't decided which.

My despair grew those last few days in Italy. I spent the time packing while contemplating rehab and quitting the show. I needed a time-out. Some rest.

I wasn't going to get it.

"Great news!"

I had begun to realize that when producers started with "Great news!" it rarely was. This time was no different. "You just got green-lit for another season!" they told us. "We're going straight to Jersey!" That phrase—"going straight to Jersey"—would become a running joke amongst the cast, one that's still going strong today.

It was the last thing I wanted to hear. I didn't even know if I wanted to do the show anymore, let alone film another season with no break. And when they said "straight to Jersey," they meant straight to Jersey.

Upon landing, we exited the airport, and they took us directly to a McDonald's for breakfast. From there, we were whisked right to the shore house. No stops, no break. Not even a single night at home. Straight to the shore house to start filming season five. I didn't know how I was going to do it.

I remember sitting in that McDonald's parking lot and not being able to eat. Everyone else was so happy to be in the States, enjoying a sense of normalcy under the golden arches. But I felt like a caged animal in the back of that van. My anxiety was through the roof. At the same time, there was a light at the end of the tunnel. I was back on my home turf where I had some sense of control. I was relieved—no, elated—to be back in Jersey, where I knew I could contact one of my boys and score the pills I so desperately needed.

It wouldn't be easy. I was being watched like a hawk 24/7. Still, I was optimistic I would somehow figure out a way to complete this mission. Despite that clause remaining in my contract threatening to take my money if I pulled any more disappearing acts, that was exactly what I planned to do. I *had* to reup my opiate supply. I was an addict. Survival was the only priority. I would do whatever it took to no longer feel this way.

Back in New Jersey, though far from free, my brain and body lit up with the possibility of the physical and mental relief offered by finally getting more pills. Any considerations of rehab and quitting the show would have to wait.

CHAPTER 17

THE ULTIMATUM

What's that? You'd like to start this chapter with another escape? Well, The Situation always gives the people what they want. As we know, production continued to be frustrated while on high alert for my tricks. They had no doubt I was constantly copping drugs yet remained unable to catch me red-handed. As we traveled directly from the airport to the shore house and went right into filming the next season, the cat and mouse game was on. My wheels began spinning as I tried to concoct a plan to evade the measures production had put in place to stop me from scoring. It's funny, no one said a word, but we all knew what was going on.

Being back on home soil, I knew it was only a matter of time before I figured out a resupply. I went to the producers, explaining that after being in Italy away from my friends and family for two months, I was homesick. If they wouldn't allow us to sleep in our own beds for a night or even stop off at home, they should at least allow me to bring home to me. I needed new clothes and shoes for the season, so I told them my brother Marc would bring all my new gear to the shore house, and then we'd go out for lunch. Begrudgingly, they allowed it.

For some reason, production thought Marc was my drug source. That couldn't have been further from the truth. Marc hates drugs, has never done them, and looked at it as part of his job to keep me from getting and doing drugs. I used that misnomer to my advantage, almost utilizing Marc as a diversion. When he came to bring me my new clothes, security was all over him and the bags, thoroughly searching them all. They paid little attention to my boy Johnny The Unit, whom I had called on the side and invited to come with Marc. Since I was always mic'd and being filmed, I had to speak in code on the phone. "Make sure you bring those girls to the club," I instructed. He knew what I meant.

When Marc and The Unit arrived, I convinced production to let the three of us go to lunch. They smelled a rat and gave me grief about it but eventually had to let us go. Of course, they sent a full camera crew and one of the top producers along in an attempt to keep me from doing what we all knew I was going to do.

As the three of us ate on the boardwalk, covered from all angles by cameras, producers, security, and cops, the scrutiny started to get to me. With relief seemingly in my grasp, I was climbing the walls. I just needed some separation from all these people to achieve the inevitable handoff with Unit.

When Marc got up from the table to use the bathroom, I saw it as my chance. Remember, I had to hide this from my brother too. With everyone watching, I gave Unit *the look*, then in code said something like, "Where those girls at?" In response, he mumbled quietly, barely audible, "Not with me."

Inwardly, I groaned. *What the fuck?!* I was pissed he didn't have them on him. He said quickly, "I left my bag in the car." Okay. At least I knew where they were.

The Unit had driven Marc's Range Rover to the shore, while Marc had come in my new Ferrari. I had a little ritual back then. After every season wrapped, I'd buy myself a new luxury car or two. That was my thing. I worked constantly and was always so busy and worn out that to make myself feel better, I'd drive all my different cars whenever I was home. By this point, the fleet had grown to a ridiculous and impractical size, especially considering I still lived in Marc's townhouse. I had all these cars lined up on his cul-de-sac: a Bentley, two Ferraris, two Lamborghinis, a BMW M5, a Porsche 911 Turbo, and a souped-up Jeep with TVs and PlayStation in the back. I hadn't even seen my new Ferrari yet, let alone driven it. Marc had taken it to the shore house so I could finally get a glimpse of my latest ride for a little motivation to complete this new season.

Now that I knew reinforcements were just a few blocks away, stashed in my brother's Range Rover, I began to climb the walls. How was I going to get the package? I needed to create some breathing room.

Next thing I knew, the producers told me we had to wrap up lunch and get back to the house. They had heard our little coded conversation and suspected something was up. They wanted to get me back to their controlled environment. I used it to my advantage.

"Yo, I was locked down in Italy for two fucking months, and you guys won't even let me go home for a single day? Now you're trying to cut short lunch with my brother and friend? Fuck that! I'm a human. I need y'all to leave me alone for a minute. Just gimme some space!"

It was a reasonable request, so it served well as a cover. What could they do? The show was doing great. They could come after my money if I bolted, but I figured I had some leeway. Besides, I didn't have a choice. I was going to do whatever it took to feel better, consequences be damned.

As soon as the producers pushed back, I went on my bullshit. Just like in Miami, I took off my mic and threw it. Just like before, I started walking, slowly at first, then picking up speed. Just like before, a crew of producers, security guards, and cops followed at a reasonable distance. It was like a hostage situation—they didn't want to get too close while calling after me, trying to de-escalate the situation. I just kept yelling at everyone, "Give me some space!"

Our little parade reached the shore house. The new red Ferrari was parked at the curb behind Marc's Range Rover. My gaze completely bypassed my new car—I had a one-track mind. Hopping in the Range Rover, I locked the doors as everyone surrounded it, shouting at me while continuing to film.

Suddenly, I had a sinking feeling. *Shit, what have I done? They're going to take my money now.* The thought quickly went away. I opened up the center console. There, looking back up at me, shimmering like a pot of gold at the end of a rainbow, was the wonderous sight of a hundred pack of Blues, the code name in the streets for thirty-milligram Roxicets. Hallelujah. It was like the heavens opened up. Pretty sure I heard violins, a chorus of angels. Maybe some doves flew overhead.

I scanned the growing crowd to see if any cops were looking inside the car. They seemed focused on the hundreds, if not thousands, of fans who were always milling about the shore house, trying to catch a glimpse of one of us. They'd spotted me getting in the Range Rover, and the mob began to encircle the car. The police stepped in to hold the crowd back, unsure what I was going to do next. Chaos reigned in the streets. It was a spectacle as the masses tried to get a better look at me in the car and crowded closer.

Luckily for me, the cops were in damage control mode, more worried about a potential riot than they were with what I was doing. I threw six or seven pills in my mouth, jocked the rest of the package next to my package, then jumped out of the car like nothing had happened. I clapped my hands and grinned at everyone.

"Aight, I'm good. Just needed a minute to catch my breath," I said, walking past the throng and into the house, now prepared to start filming the next season of *Jersey Shore* with my castmates.

And that was it. New season, same shit. *Groundhog Day*. Back to ripping and running amok. But now, a new substance had been added to my repertoire: Lean. Lean is promethazine and codeine that I mixed with Sprite. It has sedative properties while heightening the effects of the Blues I was already taking. I fell in love with Lean and began sipping on it whenever I could get my hands on a bottle. Mixed with my normal dosage of Roxicet, this was a powerful concoction that would often knock me out after gigs. It became a ritual when I traveled. I'd pop six Roxys, order room service and a movie, then mix my promethazine and codeine with Sprite and get high as hell.

I began racking up bills for burnt hotel couches when I'd pass out and the Marlboro Light dangling from my mouth invariably fell onto the furniture. Small holes would often be overlooked by hotel staff, but one time I woke up in the Gansevoort in New York City to flames on what I would learn was a twelve-thousand-dollar couch. The one I burned up in the Four Seasons in LA cost $18k. I paid for both after my attorney informed me I would be facing a lawsuit otherwise, though restitution didn't stop both establishments from banning me from their properties.

Along with the Lean, my opiate appetite had reached a new high (or low, depending on how you looked at it). I was now taking ten thirty-milligram Oxys at a time, three times a day. Enough to kill an elephant. Or at least to keep The Sitch high. At that rate, those hundred packs from The Unit wouldn't last long. Like always, a new caper needed to be drawn up.

That season, if you heard me on the phone asking someone how many girls were coming to the club, chances are I was talking with one of my boys from home in code. "Girls" meant pills, and the numbers equated to increments of ten. So, for example, if The Unit told me he was bringing five girls to the club that night, I knew I was getting a fifty pack.

Again, to be clear, Johnny Unit wasn't a drug dealer. He would just help facilitate my order. I'd ask him to meet up in the real world with one of my drug dealers, where he'd take consignment of my shipment, then deliver it to me at the club.

Once we established a code and rendezvous, the next trick would be the handoff. Easier said than done. MTV assigned an army to watch over me that season. It was a joke with the rest of the cast. We'd walk down the boardwalk, me out front of course, while thousands of tourists and locals lined the beach, chasing us and screaming our names. That was an ongoing challenge—everywhere went, fans would flock to us while we tried to ignore them and go about production. Five or six security guards typically surrounded me, leaving the rest of the roommates on their own. Pauly or someone would usually laugh, "Yep, they're sticking close to Mike for when he bolts again."

When we reached the club, the eyeballs on me only increased. It didn't matter where we went—it was always mayhem. As soon as we walked in, everyone in the place stopped and crowded around us. The DJ usually shouted out something like, *"Jersey Shore* in the building!" How could the handoff happen when half the club—plus *all* the security—was watching me like a hawk? Not to mention the omnipresent cameras and the fact that I was wearing a microphone.

The bathroom seemed like the most logical spot, but producers even went in there with me carrying handheld cameras. It was impossible to be alone unless I went into a stall and locked the door. Obviously, production wasn't going to allow someone to come into the stall with me. So here's what we did:

The plan called for one of my boys from home to get close enough to make eye contact with me but not greet me. With just that look, it was on. We knew what to do. I would make my way to the bathroom, cameras and all in tow. My boy, whether it be Tommy, Unit, or whoever, would get in line a few people in front of me, still without acknowledging me. They'd go into a stall and wrap toilet paper around a piece of tinfoil holding fifty or a hundred pills, drop it on the nasty Jenks or Bamboo floor, and exit the bathroom without so much as looking at me. I'd make sure to use that stall. Though I was still mic'd, the camera didn't follow me in. I'd bend down, pick up the ball of toilet paper from the sticky club bathroom floor that no one in their right mind would touch, and I'd have my reup.

We pulled that feat almost every time we went to the club in season five. I wasn't worried about someone else unsuspectingly picking up my package off the floor—who was going to grab bundled toilet paper from the floor of a nightclub bathroom?

In the end, I made it through another season relatively unscathed, riding this somehow still cresting wave of sex, drugs, and reality TV. *Jersey Shore* continued to be a cultural phenomenon. The ratings were through the roof. We're talking *Game of Thrones* numbers. The Italy season premiere had 8.79 million viewers. *Jersey Shore* was the most-watched show in MTV history with episodes rivaling viewership of major network shows. Our ratings bonuses were regularly half a million dollars. Not bad for a young guido from Staten Island. My shooting star had been rising for so long that I forgot what goes up must come down. But the show's success kept me propped up a little longer—if not for that, The Situation would have already flamed out.

I kept pushing the envelope with MTV. I didn't like their rules or lockdown protocols and threw my weight around whenever I saw an opportunity. It was that cat and mouse game I referenced earlier, and they didn't like that the mouse kept winning. The only reason I got away with my behavior was because the show continued to be a juggernaut. I figured I had some control—MTV wasn't going to risk losing the face of their monster hit.

Were they?

Everyone reaches a breaking point, and I finally found MTV's. Despite the ratings and money I was making for the network, they'd had enough. After final interviews that season, I raced off in my Ferrari instead of allowing them to film my exit. They were pissed.

I was told later that the police detail responsible for securing our sets was instructed to pull me over. It was hinted that if they searched me, they were sure to find drugs. I hadn't even made it to the bridge leading out of town two blocks from the house when a Seaside police cruiser raced up behind me, lights on.

"Hold on a second, Sitch," the cop who pulled me over said before walking back to his cruiser. I could see him talking on the phone. I had no idea what was going on, but I knew my fate hung in the balance. If he searched me, I was done. Possession, jail, public humiliation. I'd probably get fired from the show too. But honestly, my hubris prevented me from really worrying about those very realistic outcomes. Finally, after a few minutes, the officer walked back to my car.

"Alright, Sitch, get home safe," he said, tapping my roof and smiling. Once again, I got off scot-free. That's just the way it was for me.

Or so I thought. Shortly after that, MTV gave me an ultimatum: Go to rehab and come back clean before season six starts filming. If not, The Situation that America fell in love and hate with would be out of a job.

I remember thinking, *alright, fair enough*. I was actually surprised they had let me take it this far. I was just happy they hadn't fired me—yet. I knew my antics were blatant and anti-authority. I broke every rule they had. I was disrespectful to my fellow cast members and the crew and exuded a sense of entitlement. I wasn't pleasant to be around. And it was all a result of my drug use.

The truth is I had no illusions about how badly I needed rehab. I wanted to detox in a medical facility under the care of professionals. My employer's threat just greased the wheels, and I readily agreed to go to a rehab facility and get clean. I didn't want to lose my job, and honestly, I was tiring of the lifestyle. I needed to make changes.

After a nerve-racking incident during that season, I went so far as to distance myself from Johnny The Unit, my close friend who was battling his own demons. I love the guy; we had grown up together, traveled the world, and always looked out for each other, but we were gasoline and fire. I knew if he stayed in my life, nothing would change for either of us.

After a night at Karma, Unit and I had brought some girls back to the shore house. Standard protocol is whenever anyone enters the house while we're filming, they have to fill out paperwork and get frisked. The Unit must have been so high he forgot he had ketamine in his pocket. Security found it and handed him over to the Seaside police, who always had a presence on set.

This was bad. The cat had finally gotten the mouse. My buddy getting busted by the company that paid my bills felt like the final sign that a major transformation was no longer negotiable. The heat from MTV was getting hotter, and I *wanted* to get sober. But first, I had a two-week tour in Australia to endure.

Once again, rehab would have to take a backseat to business.

CHAPTER 18

REHAB (#2)

What? You want *another* chase? Not sick of them by now? Aight, here's two for ya. Australia. Season five had just wrapped. I was at the end of my rope. This shooting star was fizzling. On its way back down to Earth, headed for a spectacular explosion. Mercifully, I knew I was getting help after this jaunt down under. MTV had dictated treatment, and I was still on board just as soon as this series of nightclub appearances concluded. All I had to do was make it that far.

Truthfully, I was in no shape to make the trip. A tour was the last thing I needed, but I couldn't turn down the money. They were paying me $30k a night to show up at nightclubs and take photos. Some nights, there were multiple events. In this business, you've got to strike while the iron is hot. Who knew how long my fifteen minutes would last? I had to take advantage while I could.

When we landed in Australia, my whole team headed directly to the hotel to get settled in and prepare for the first event that night. I had other plans. Even with everyone keyed on me, watching my every step, I managed to give them the slip. I put a bug in the ear of the main promoter, a healthy-looking woman. I told her what I needed, and she said she'd try to take care of it. The two of us stealthily bounced without telling anyone, and the search was on.

This promoter led me through some shady Australian neighborhoods, visiting various drug dealers she knew, trying to find Oxys. Back at the hotel, my team was freaking out, calling everyone to let them know they'd lost me again. They were understandably dumbfounded that I'd managed to escape and was missing. As someone said on our family chat, "How do you lose one of the most famous people in the world?" It would have been funny if not so dire.

For hours, they searched for me. For those same hours, this promoter and I searched the seediest parts of the city for opiates. Finally, success was ours. We scored some Oxy eighties, which I popped before arriving at the hotel. The pills looked old and crusty, but I was so happy she came through for me that we started to hook up. Next thing I knew, she was on her knees. When I reconnected with my team, I acted like nothing had happened and started to get ready for that night's appearance.

Over the next two weeks while we toured Australia, I was so strung out and tired I could barely pull myself out of bed. I only had to work a few hours each night, from about 11:00 p.m. to 2:00 a.m., but even that was a struggle. I showed up late. I tried to cancel appearances. It was a disaster. My team literally had to dress me each night and drag me to the events.

I was in rough shape. I wasn't healthy. I'd gained weight and didn't look good. Somehow though, I made it through that appearance tour. Thankfully, it was time to head back to the States to get the help I desperately needed. I had a direct flight from Australia to Utah, where I would immediately check into Cirque Lodge, an exclusive rehab facility in the Rocky Mountains. But before our flight left, I needed to make a quick stop.

Walking through the airport, withdrawals making each step more excruciating than the last, I was unsure how I was going to survive a twenty-hour flight with no pills. Suddenly, I spotted a pharmacy. I couldn't believe my fortune. On the fly, a plan began to take shape.

As my whole team—and the rest of the flight's passengers—boarded the aircraft, I jumped out of line and made a dash for that pharmacy. It took my people maybe a minute before they turned to each other, confused, like, *Where's Mike?*

While they sat on the plane, trying to figure out how they'd lost me again, I reached the pharmacy. I breathlessly explained to the pharmacist that I had run out of my medicine and needed a refill. They knew who I was and asked what medicine I was taking.

"Oxy," I answered.

"Okay, what strength?"

"The strongest you got."

"The highest dosage we have is ten milligrams," the pharmacist said. "But you'll need a prescription. All you have to do is go to the airport doctor upstairs, and they can call it down."

Perfect. I took off, sprinting through the airport in search of the small clinic she had provided directions to. Keep in mind, our flight had completed boarding and my absence was delaying departure. My team was on board freaking out, not sure what to do about their missing charge.

When I got in front of the doctor, I made an impassioned and truthful plea. "I ran out of my prescription," I told him, "and if I don't get more, I'm going to get violently ill on this flight."

It took some convincing, but finally, he called down to the pharmacy with a script for ten-milligram Oxys. Not as potent as I was used to, but they would do the trick. I sprinted through the airport, back to the pharmacy, ignoring the calls, texts, and intercom pages, aware but uncaring that I was holding this entire flight up. When I reached the pharmacy, they handed me the pill bottle like a baton; I took it in stride, continuing my sprint through the terminal.

As I neared my gate, I swear it was like a movie. *Rocky* or some shit. All these Australians were lined up on each side of the terminal, cheering me on as I ran. It was like the finish line of a marathon, and as I broke the victory tape and boarded the plane, I felt a rush of relief through the sweat and my pounding heart. I promptly took my seat and popped the entire bottle of pills, enjoying the trip home high as a kite.

I arrived at rehab feeling pretty good. Not dope sick at least. But more than that, I felt optimistic. Like this was the fresh start I needed. Furthermore, I realized I was actually happy. Happy to be there. Happy to be happy. The stay meant abiding by MTV's wishes while at the same time placing myself in the care of doctors and nurses who would be able to soften the withdrawals and crash that were to come. Mostly, I was happy to be finally getting a rest.

Cirque Lodge is a super high-end, pristine facility with beautiful panoramic views of snow-capped mountains and majestic pines. Walking in and taking in my new surroundings, I felt amazing. Sensations of promise and hope ran down my body for the first time in a long time. The crisp altitudinal air helped me breathe easier. *God, this is exactly what I need*, I thought as I soaked in the amazing vistas from every room in the facility. I felt, literally, on top of the world.

Until suddenly, I wasn't. Before my treatment journey at Cirque Lodge could even really begin, my team learned that someone at the center had leaked my stay. Every news outlet was reporting that The Situation had checked into the facility. They described where I was and what I was doing there. I was crushed. I couldn't help but feel that my recovery had been robbed by some asshole violating my HIPAA rights.

I felt like I had no choice but to leave rehab once the news broke. My best friend, Pete, who worked for me, along with a doctor and nurse, snuck me out the back of the facility in two blacked-out SUVs to throw off any paparazzi lurking outside or hiding in the woods. My team made plans to bring me to a secret location where I could detox in peace.

I knew how badly I needed this. I just wanted to be left alone and get it done. But it wasn't meant to be. The whole violation of my privacy upset me quite a bit, but it was par for the course. That was my life. Usually, I had no issues with the downsides of fame, but in times like this, it was disappointing that my personal space was nonexistent. Instead of detoxing and completing an intensive rehab at a top-notch facility, I had to figure out treatment on my own.

We ended up renting a beautiful log cabin in the mountains near Cirque Lodge, which allowed me to still detox under medical supervision amid the scenery and falling snow; however, without a holistic treatment center, I could only focus on the physical parts of my addiction. I was able to physically kick opiates, but recovery is so much more than that. I still had no idea that the mental and spiritual aspects were equally as important as the physical.

After seven to ten days enduring a brutal medical detox amongst the whispering aspen pines of Utah's ski country, I still felt horrible. But the drugs had left my body and I was getting better every day. It was time to complete my comeback.

MTV told me I'd better return to the set for the next season like The Situation had arrived in season one—sober and with a six-pack. After all, you can't really have the nickname I had and not be in peak condition. I'd completed their first requirement by going to rehab. Getting camera-ready would meet their second. I was itching to start recrafting my body.

Despite the continued mental anguish inherent in only partially treating my addiction, with my system drug free, I was able to start working out again. It would take many baby steps before becoming camera-ready, but I was on my way. Two-a-days became the norm as I spent at least three hours a day in the gym alternating between weights and cardio, only taking off one day a week. There wasn't much time before shooting started, but I was ready to get back to work—physically, at least.

CHAPTER 19

WINTER IS COMING

U pon returning to Jersey, untethered from the yoke of opiates for the first time in years, I was a man on a mission—clean, sober, and determined to get in fighting shape for the new season of *Jersey Shore*. Not just figuratively.

Pete was also a boxing trainer, so I hired him to train me on the roof of the shore house every morning during filming. We started at 7:00 a.m., getting in a good hour in the sun, sweating and working our asses off before the rest of the cast woke up. The roommates saw my renewed dedication to fitness and training, and it sent them subtle a message: I meant business this season and was willing to put the work in.

My motivation for showing up to season six in the best shape of my life was twofold. Yeah, I wanted to look great and show the world The Situation was back, but I also thought I had some unfinished business with Ronnie. I felt like he'd gotten the best of me in our scrap in Italy, and there was a disrespect that I needed to address.

My solution was to get completely shredded. I wanted to walk into that season looking like the Hulk. For the first time ever, I decided to solicit some help to get there. I'd never done steroids before—had never needed them—but for this mission, I went all in, injecting myself with a cocktail of high-powered performance-enhancing drugs: tren, test, equipoise, winstrol…a who's who of anabolic steroids. For someone still coping with newfound sobriety and recovering from the mental trauma of years of opiate abuse, this was a dangerous mix.

As it was, my mental state was already precarious. I didn't realize it then, but it's very difficult to control your emotions early on in recovery. For years, chemical dependency had allowed me to bury pain and trauma through a fog of drugs; now that those chemicals had been removed, all the emotions came rushing to the surface. Combining a toxic potpourri of steroids was like adding fuel to the fire. My anger was through the roof. I was ready to throw down and fight at a moment's notice, and you saw a lot of that during the final season of *Jersey Shore*. And there was a lot more you didn't see on TV, incidents production edited out after security had to hold me back from going after people at the club.

To help keep me sober, I elected to get a Vivitrol shot. Vivitrol blocks the pleasure receptors in the brain from feeling the effects of alcohol and opiates, so even if I suffered a momentary loss of willpower, drinking or taking Oxy would have no effect on me.

However, shockingly, when I told the prescribing doctor—who KNEW I had just been released from rehab for abusing prescription pills—that I was suffering from low energy, he inexplicably gave me a script for Adderall, which is an amphetamine. For a recovering pill head, that was the absolute worst thing he could have done. Adderall would lead me down a pit of evil that would take years to crawl out of. I call the time period spent under the spell of Adderall "The Dark Years." Like in *Game of Thrones*, winter was coming. I would completely lose my mind during the years I abused Adderall.

For starters, do you think I followed the instructions on the bottle saying to take one pill per day? Fuck no! I'm an addict! I popped them like candy. *Hmm, I wonder what this will do?* was my mindset. Instead of allowing my brain to heal from the years of opiate damage, I was now feeding it a new drug—speed—which opened up a whole new world of paranoia and anxiety. I mean, I heard voices that weren't there. To exacerbate matters, when I told my doctor the Adderall got me too high and speedy and I was having trouble sleeping, this guy wrote me a script for Valium. Another narcotic to abuse.

But MTV was happy. I showed up for filming looking amazing. I was jacked and appeared healthy. As far as they were concerned, The Situation was clean and sober. I wasn't drinking or taking opiates; in fact, my drugs were now considered legal medicine, prescribed under the care of a licensed physician. I didn't have to hide my pill bottles this time, and production took me to get my monthly Vivitrol shot.

They didn't know about the steroids or that I was back to my old tricks acting as my own chemist. Adderall in the morning for my workout, but then, I'd feel too speedy, so I started rolling joints in the bathroom and smoking weed to calm down. Valium at night to sleep. Not to mention a constant stream of Red Bulls and Marlboro Lights throughout the day. Once again, I was a walking pharmacy; I'd merely substituted new drugs for old.

That season was tough on me. I was doing my best to make amends with the cast for my past behavior—especially Snooki—but it wasn't easy. I had a lot to make up for. I tried to show the roommates that I was a good person with a good heart and that I wanted to revive our friendships, but I recognized it would take time to repair those relationships. I was trying to be better and to do the right things. They didn't buy in right away, but at least they could tell I was trying. Still, my efforts didn't mean we were suddenly all best friends again.

My head was still in a terrible spot, and my attempt at sobriety was at best trial and error—with a lot of error. This new concoction of drugs made me super paranoid. I made more mistakes as I fought through waves of depression and struggled with my mental health. I didn't realize it at the time, but I was only fighting myself (and losing the battle).

At least the drama with Ronnie didn't continue. I'd come into that season ready for combat, though I was determined not to start anything. I was tired of being the villain and wasn't going to purposefully do anything to give my roommates more of a reason to hate me. Again, I wanted the opposite—to earn my way back into their good graces. So I never pushed the envelope with Ronnie, nor did he with me. In fact, the vibe between us that season was respectful and nonconfrontational. I think Vinny, Pauly, and Ron saw how much work I had put into improving myself, and the boys respected me for taking steps in the right direction.

In the middle of filming, the producers dropped what should have been a bomb on us. But the truth is, when the network informed us that this was to be the last season of *Jersey Shore*, none of us were fazed. Production declared that with the ratings still strong, they wanted to close on a high note. I think they saw how tired we all were and viewed this as a good way to go out on top. The squad and I were in agreement.

Everyone had side projects and spinoff deals, and we figured we wouldn't miss a beat once *Jersey Shore* was off the air.

Besides, MTV was right. We were all beyond exhausted, and I think we looked at the show's end as an opportunity to catch our breath and figure out the next chapter of our lives. No one was worried. Big checks were still coming in. With all the money each of us had accumulated during this run of monster success, we could afford to take a little break. I certainly looked at the news as an opportunity to finally get the rest I'd wanted for so long. The show had been a wild ride, but it didn't mean the journey was over.

I had a spinoff deal with MTV already in my contract. It wasn't *Jersey Shore* money, but $72,000 an episode to film a Situation-centric show wasn't bad. I figured after the final season ended, I'd go immediately to the MTV offices and they'd green-light my own show. The network seemed to be of the same mindset, but when I pitched a Sorrentino family show, they balked at the idea. I guess MTV had a bad taste in their mouth and were not exactly fans of working with my family. In the end, creative differences forced me to become a free agent, and we did the show on another network a couple years later.

Not moving immediately into production on another reality show with MTV didn't concern me. The Situation business wasn't slowing. Instead, we went straight into the next thing, like we always did. That big goodbye group hug in the street outside the shore house on the final episode gave me no sense of finality. I had no doubt I would see all my castmates again in some capacity. A connection like that doesn't fade. Despite all the fights and drama, the eight of us were tied together for life through this amazing experience. Together, we had garnered record ratings and become a pop culture marvel. We knew it would somehow continue.

In fact, that rest I was hoping for didn't happen right away. Instead, after filming for *Jersey Shore* wrapped, I made an immediate trip to the UK to film *Celebrity Big Brother* and then embarked on a European nightclub tour. As always, travels to other countries weren't good for me.

I was still heavy into Adderall and Valium, and now that I was no longer under MTV's control while also away from my doctors in the US, I had stopped taking the Vivitrol shot. Vivitrol wears off if you don't get it every month, and I relapsed on opiates. Before long, I was back to my old tricks. During the filming of *Celebrity Big Brother* UK, I faked an injury after a challenge and got the network doctor to prescribe me Hydrocodone. Hydrocodone is a weaker opiate than I was used to, but since I'd been clean of opiates for about a year, my tolerance was low.

Now that they had a taste, the demons in my head began screaming louder and louder for more. I urgently began seeking what they wanted. *Big Brother* was over, and the UK nightclub tour commenced, meaning the debauchery ramped up. Again, it was a life of sex, drugs, and selfies. But my drug of choice was hard to come by in England, so I made do with copious amounts of alcohol, weed, Adderall, Valium, and increasingly, MDMA. Once again, I was playing chemist. My addiction and dependency worse than ever, I barely made it through those UK appearances.

But somehow, as always, I did. Upon arriving home, my state of mind did not improve. Begging for a rest, I basically locked myself in the house. I didn't want to be seen. I didn't want to be bothered. I wanted to do drugs and be left alone. I became a recluse.

I was depressed. I was in the midst of two lawsuits, one of which was with my previous employer. After years of me using the term "GTL" in the branding and marketing of products I sold, MTV and their parent company Viacom said not so fast, and a battle ensued over the trademark. In the end, even though the court acknowledged the moniker had been created by me and Pauly in season one, it was ruled we had done so as employees of Viacom. Therefore, I couldn't own the term, but I was allowed to use it. The worst part of the suit, aside from the additional stress, was the money wasted on lawyers.

The other lawsuit stemmed from a press release Abercrombie & Fitch put out saying they were going to pay me $10,000 *not* to wear their clothes. They hilariously claimed that me wearing some Abercrombie sweats on the show was hurting their brand. As far as I know, they never actually made me the offer they claimed they had—if so, I would have taken it. I don't turn down free money! But no offer ever reached me, and at the end of the day, it was a brilliant publicity stunt that ended up doing exactly what they wanted it to—ride my wave of fame without paying me for it. They claimed I was tarnishing their brand by wearing their clothes, yet they began to sell a "Fitchuation" T-shirt, basically using my name without my permission and without compensating me.

We sued them for trademark infringement, unfair competition, false advertising, injury to business reputation, and misappropriation of likeness. To me, the case was a slam dunk. They'd done all those things. But a judge didn't see it that way and ruled against us. I thought we caught a raw deal and honestly am still pretty pissed about it to this day. But I choose to be better, not bitter, living by the adage, "Do not seek revenge; the rotten fruits will fall by themselves." I think it's safe to say that fruit has long since fallen. Is A&F even around anymore?

These losses and massive legal fees took their toll, both mentally and financially. My family was worried about me. They saw my addiction for what it was: a one-way ticket to death. There seemed to be no light at the end of this tunnel. I think the people around me were beginning to realize that there was no coming back from this. I hate to say it, but people started to give up on me. And why shouldn't they? I had given up on myself.

There was only one person who could offer a glimmer of hope. Who could save me or at least give me the motivation to save myself. Someone I hadn't talked to in a couple of years but who was never far from my mind.

So when my sister called me and said she had bumped into Lauren, I felt a sense of optimism for the first time in years.

CHAPTER 20

RECONCILIATION AND LOSS

"I went to this boxing class at a gym in Freehold," my sister was saying, "and guess who was there?"

I felt the hair stand up on the back of my neck. Intuition suggested the answer, but I wanted to hear her say it.

"Who...?" I asked hopefully.

"Lauren!" she answered with excitement.

As I said, my family was extremely concerned about me. Lauren had been the last positive influence in my life, and everyone had faith she could help me turn my life around. I shared that confidence. As someone who believes wholeheartedly in fate, I felt this encounter was more than chance—rather, a sign from above. An outstretched hand offering assistance at the time I needed it the most. I was going to do everything I could to take advantage of it.

Leading up to this, I cared about nothing. I simply wanted to be left alone to do drugs and not feel anything. Not only was my brain dependent on these chemicals, but I was so famous that I couldn't go outside or into a store. I was tired of taking selfies and FaceTime-ing people's relatives on the street. I felt like an animal trapped in a cage.

Each week, thousands of dollars went to pills. Imagine trying to be inconspicuous while driving a white Lamborghini on twenty-inch Forgiato rims to a drug dealer's house. I would go home, get high, and watch movies surrounded by all my favorite foods, snacks, and an excess of McDonald's or other fast food. That was my life. It was obviously a miserable existence.

But when I heard about my sister seeing Lauren, a sense of optimism and hope crept into my brain for the first time in a long time. I was actually thinking of something other than drugs, food, money, or fame. I peppered Melissa with questions: *Where? When? How did she look?* When

135

she told me it had been at an 8:00 p.m. class at CKO Kickboxing in Freehold Township, I immediately decided that I would be in attendance at the same time the next day in the hopes of running into her.

It worked. There she was. As beautiful as ever. She looked exactly the same as I remembered. Smiling, glowing. Our eyes met across the room, and it was like time hadn't passed. There was an immediate spark. It was as if the four years that had gone by since we'd last seen each other didn't exist.

After the kickboxing class, we went to my car to talk. Our chemistry was still palpable. She let me know that things weren't working out with her boyfriend. They were supposed to get engaged soon, but the relationship was no longer moving in that direction. She wanted a family, and it turned out he was not who she thought he was. We ended up kissing and exchanging numbers that night. Soon, we picked up right where we left off.

Reconnecting with Lauren was a gift from above. I truly believe a higher power placed her back in my life at exactly the moment when I needed her the most. She was the push that brought me back from the edge of death—because that's what I was doing, slowly killing myself. I was never suicidal, but there was no doubt that with the way I was pushing the limits of the human body, I wasn't long for this world. When you do drugs like I was, you don't love yourself. You're addicted, you're dependent, and there's little self-respect there. I'd lost my way in life, and once Lauren was back in the picture, it felt like I'd found whatever it was I'd been searching for. I went from not having an interest in anything to waking up every morning excited for life because the love of my life was back in it.

This doesn't mean I was suddenly healed. Far from it. I was still very sick. Nowhere close to my best self. I tried to hide my addiction from Lauren, or at least excuse it to a certain extent by explaining that all these pills were from a doctor, but she didn't buy it. She could see that I didn't look good and was harming myself. I mean, my regimen of narcotics was still crazy. Adderall in the morning to wake up. Roxy and weed throughout the day. Valium at night. I didn't drink much because

I'd never been a big fan of alcohol, usually only using it to help with withdrawals. On the show, it often looked like I was drinking, but that cocktail in my hand was really just a prop. In reality, I was intoxicated on everything else.

These habits were not good for my newly rekindled relationship. Still, Lauren and I were making it work because, despite my issues, the two of us were madly in love. But around me, life continued unraveling. In order to keep the business going, I did more endorsements and appearances. I was still hot and had to take advantage while I could, no matter how sick and tired I was.

The pharmaceutical company that makes Suboxone, the drug that decreases the severity of withdrawal symptoms while reducing your dependence on opioids, approached my team. They wanted to give me like half a million dollars to be the main brand ambassador for this drug and inspire heroin and Oxy addicts to get clean. You can't make this shit up. Here I was, a raging opiate addict, taking like thirty Roxicet a day, and they wanted me to rep the antidote to those drugs.

I remember sitting in that first meeting with their executives, wondering if they could tell I was high. They discussed the entire campaign, the commercials and everything, as I sat there thinking, *This is crazy. I can't get sober to save my life, and I'm going to be the face of this drug? How ironic is this?*

But it paid well, and so I went through the motions pimping Suboxone. For a year, I did the commercials and made the speeches while consuming the drug their product was supposed to help you stop taking. I did a pretty poor job as a spokesperson if I'm being honest. I was too high to take it seriously. An endorsement deal wasn't going to motivate me to get clean. I was too far gone for that.

But I had to keep the revenue coming in. Too many people depended on me for their livelihood. Except for my dad, my entire family worked for the entertainment company that kept The Situation machine running, and I paid them all healthy salaries. I'm old school, and I took this responsibility seriously. It all added up to hundreds of thousands of dollars a year in expenses. I received *Jersey Shore* residuals, but when the show ended, the per episode fees went with it. It was taking longer than I expected to sell the family show. So when an opportunity came for an appearance tour in Spain, there was no hesitation. Again, in my state, international travel was horrible for me, but also again, I had to strike when the iron was hot.

It's what I did for a living. I endorsed things. I went on TV shows. I did appearances. I moved from one thing to another to maintain me and my family's lifestyle. No one forced me to do those things; I wanted to. I was in demand, and I didn't know when that would change. So to pay the bills, I accepted these challenges despite the toll they took on me.

Before I left, things started to get even more crazy. We got word that a federal investigation into how the business was being run was underway. Several people who worked for me had been served with subpoenas. The feds showed up at the home of Pete, who was my CFO, as well as Marc's house. No one knew exactly what was going on, but it seemed like a grand jury indictment for tax crimes was about to come down. Hell was breaking loose around me, all while I raced around town scoring as many painkillers as possible to smuggle into Spain, incognito as always in a black Porsche 911.

To repurpose another *Goodfellas* scene depicting my state of mind, I felt like Ray Liotta when he was driving around stoned on coke, looking up at the sky, trying to determine if helicopters were following him. I was that paranoid and with good reason. My phone had started to make clicking sounds, making me wonder if it was tapped. I knew I had to be next in this round of sweeping subpoenas, but I naively figured that if I could just lay low for a few days and make it to Spain without getting busted, maybe everything would go away. I started sleeping at hotels and hiding out at friends' houses until it was time to leave. I was scheduled to be in Spain for a month; I assumed the feds couldn't find me there.

I assumed wrong.

Marc, Frank, Pete, and I were sitting in the VIP lounge of Newark International Airport, waiting for our greeter to escort us to the gate. Once boarding commenced, we began that process, winding through the airport as fans snapped photos and called out to me. A hoodie was pulled low over dark sunglasses, my normal travel attire, designed to offer a modicum of privacy while also hiding the unavoidable fact that I was high as hell.

Upon arrival at the gate, in addition to the standard throng of travelers waiting to board, I noticed six or seven similar-looking dudes in suits and blue windbreakers. They seemed to be waiting for us. Through the fog of intoxication, alarm bells started to go off in my head. *Is this it? The big bust?* I wasn't sure what I had done wrong; I didn't even know the details of my own business—how could they arrest me for that?

Protectively, my team stood in a row in front of me, forming a wall between the agents and me. I felt like Al Capone. My bag was full of illegal prescription drugs. If they searched me, I was done.

But the agents essentially ignored me. I remained in the background, hoping they would leave me alone. I couldn't even hear what they said to my team. All I saw was one of them hand documents to Marc. Then, they left the terminal, allowing us to board our flight to Spain.

We were in shock. What the hell was that? My team looked over the papers on the flight and saw it confirmed that we were under investigation for tax crimes. I didn't want to deal with it. I saw this as a problem for my team to navigate, ironically the same attitude responsible for getting myself in this predicament in the first place.

Upon landing in Spain, Marc and Pete immediately turned around and flew back home to deal with this new issue while Frank and I remained to complete the tour. Soon, I forgot about my legal issues, having bigger fish to fry. Like where to score pills in a foreign land once again.

The tour promoter met us at the airport. Carlos was a skinny fat, shady-looking dude with dark hair and eyes and a scruffy beard. He seemed to be into some pretty extracurricular things, and I had no trouble convincing him to go into a pharmacy and get me whatever he could. He came out with boxes of effervescent codeine, which wasn't strong enough for me to get high, though good enough to stave off withdrawals. Carlos and I would repeat these pharmacy visits several times over my stay in Spain.

By the end of that tour, my paranoia had reached epic proportions. Between the chemicals wreaking havoc on my brain, the weight of the indictments, and any energy left being spent trying to get more pills, I was in rough shape. This wasn't like previous tours. It wasn't fun for me. The time for partying was gone. Girls continued throwing themselves at me, but now I had a girlfriend back home. Things were so chaotic that I hid away in my hotel as much as possible, trying to numb myself to the madness. I just wanted to get in and out, get paid and go home.

Then, one night right before we left, Lauren called me in my hotel room. "Mike, I need you to call Chris," she said urgently. I could hear the worry and fear in her voice. Chris was her little brother, twenty-five at the time and, like me, addicted to opiates. "Please try to get ahold of him. He's not picking up. We're afraid something is wrong. He looks up to you—he'll take your call. We think he's up to no good."

I was happy to help, and Chris answered when I called. We were both going through the same thing: struggling with addiction, trying to get sober, and suffering relapses. If anyone understood his battles, it was me.

"What are you doing, man?" I asked. "Your family is worried about you. Do the right thing. Call them and let them know you're okay."

He sounded fine, like nothing was wrong. "Sure, man. Everything is good. I'm in a sober house. I'll call everyone and let them know."

I hung up feeling happy he had taken my call and content that he sounded safe and planned to call his family.

Unfortunately, the next morning, Chris was found dead in the sober living house where he was attempting to get clean. Brother, son, and friend Christopher L. Pesce died on October 13, 2013, leaving a gaping in hole in all of our hearts.

His death hit close to home. I had been the last one to speak with him, and I was going through something similar. Needless to say, Chris's passing was earth-shattering for us all. What else can you say about such a tragedy? I needed to get home and take care of my heartbroken girlfriend and also get a handle on how bad these legal issues were. It was a scary time. The wolves were at the gate. The Spain tour completed,

Frank and I made our way to the airport, more than ready for the return trip, accompanied by Carlos, the shady promoter.

As I described earlier, I got paid part of my appearance fee on these tours in cash. As a result, I had a duffel bag with tens of thousands of dollars on my person when we arrived at the airport. Carlos, who I suspected wasn't exactly all there (to be fair, neither was I), seemed to have a fixation on that duffel. It could have been the opiate come-down combined with speed (Adderall) and Xanax wrecking my brain and central nervous system, but I started to get the distinct feeling this dude was not who he was pretending to be. My already intense paranoia increased tenfold, and I became convinced that everyone in the airport was out to get me. (Remember, just because you're paranoid doesn't mean it's not true.)

Hyperalert, I clutched the bag of cash tightly, white knuckling the leather straps. Also containing my drugs, it was my lifeline, and I became more and more convinced someone was trying to take it and rob me. I got the distinct impression a nefarious plot was underway. *This promoter is setting me up. He knows how much cash is in the bag.* With Marc and Pete already back home to hire lawyers, I was rolling with a skeleton crew in a foreign country with no backup if something happened.

I began to pick up on what appeared to be spotters strategically positioned throughout the airport, scoping me out as part of this conspiracy while reporting my movements to each other over the phone. I was certain the same groups of people were following me, and no matter how hard I tried to shake them, they stayed in lockstep. I stayed as close as I could to the airline representatives after noticing two gentlemen staring intensely at me. Keep in mind, I was on a world-famous reality show as one of the main characters. Everyone recognized me wherever I went. But these dudes didn't seem like friendlies. One of them looked like the uncle from *Breaking Bad*, Hector Salamanca. Old, bald, and deadly. The other guy seemed like the muscle. Jacked, probably six-foot-three with long blond hair, like Thor. Thor had a rolled-up magazine in his hand, and all I could think was that it contained a shank. I told Frank I thought our lives were in danger, and he started panicking as well.

We arrived at the gate, and these characters who I believed were trying to harm me had stayed with us every step of the way. I remained near the airline rep until it was time to board a trolley that would take us to the plane. Thor and Salamanca lined up to get on the same trolley. This was the moment of truth. I had no doubt my life was on the line. They were on my flight, and all I could envision was them stabbing me in my sleep and taking my bag. Some diabolical scheme like that. I decided to not get on the trolley. Guess who else elected not to board?

I was like, *Oh shit, it's on.* I didn't want to overreact and do something rash, but every movement seemed to confirm my suspicions. With adrenaline and nerves pumping in overdrive, my next bright idea was to take another Adderall. Right, that was exactly what I needed—more speed. Body tingling, I went into my bag and popped another pill. I figured the amphetamines would give me some extra alertness.

By now, all the other passengers were on the plane. It was only me, Frank, Thor, and Salamanca left. The whole group got on the next trolley. I looked at Frank. I swear he had tears coming down his face. I kept my eye on Thor's rolled-up magazine and the shank I assumed he had in there, still making sure I stayed close to the airline rep. I figured if it went down here, I wanted an authority figure nearby.

I watched as Salamanca put his hand over his mouth and seemed to signal Thor with a slight headshake. Like saying it was off. Or "not here, not now." I interpreted it as they were either going to get me on the plane or wait until we landed. No fucking way was I getting on that plane after seeing that.

I looked at Frank and his quivering bottom lip. "Get your shit together," I growled softly, trying to foreshadow my next move. Then, as the trolley rolled toward the jet, I suddenly leapt off and did a tumble, rolling away like I was on some James Bond movie set. My brother, a tear rolling down his cheek, did the same. You should have seen the look of shock on the airline rep's face. *Oh my God, The Situation just did a tuck and roll onto the tarmac!* When the potential robbers reached the plane door, I saw them look back at us before entering the main cabin.

Things were chaotic, to say the least. Frank and I raced back to the hotel while also trying to find the American embassy and call our family. "Yo, you gotta switch my flight," I told Marc breathlessly. "And you gotta get me security. They're after me. I just foiled some plot where I was about to be robbed."

When Frank and I arrived in our recently vacated hotel room, now wearing disguises, it appeared to have been ransacked, confirming our suspicions that the Spaniards were indeed after us. My people called the promoter and threatened him with arrest if anything happened to me. Then, they booked Frank and I on another flight, and we safely flew home.

Was I ever in danger? Maybe. I have no idea—I was on a lot of drugs. Imagine if I did all that and they were fans who only wanted a picture? I'll never know if the plot was real or in my head, but I certainly felt like my life was in jeopardy. Either way, it's hell of a story.

CHAPTER 21

ANOTHER CHASE AND ANOTHER REHAB (#3)

My addiction continued to consume me like an out-of-control fire overtakes a dry forest. Fortunately, I received a piece of good news right when I needed it the most. Could this be the motivation I required to finally get clean once and for all? (Spoiler alert: no. But we're getting there...)

The family show I'd been pitching for the past couple of years since *Jersey Shore* ended had finally been picked up by Pop TV. *The Sorrentinos* would start filming in a couple of months. But before that happened, I would need to get in camera shape. Being continuously high was anything but conducive for health and fitness. I needed to get clean. Again.

This time, I decided to medically detox privately in my home in an effort to prevent the press and public from finding out. It was very important to me to hide my addiction from the world. Only my family knew the full extent of my demons. I didn't want people to think I was weak and know I still couldn't get it right. I assumed the perception would be that something was wrong with me. I worried that if people knew the full story, if they realized how many times I'd failed at sobriety, they would think less of me.

When you first decide to get treatment, there is some initial sympathy and support. When you go three or four times, that begins to disappear. Having failed previously, I felt a bit defeated. What I wasn't considering was the reality that most people aren't successful in their first attempts at recovery. In the recipe of success, one of the main ingredients is failure. The key is to not give up on yourself. When you come across an obstacle, you have to understand it's nothing more than a brilliantly disguised opportunity. Keep moving forward, don't give up, and eventually you'll find success. Too many people face failure and treat it like a finality. Once you meet failure, it simply means you've found a way that didn't work. Use that knowledge to find another way.

I didn't understand any of that yet.

What I did understand was that it was time for Mike to finally man up. To put on my big boy pants and do what needed to be done. I couldn't mess this up. I made a commitment to get clean for myself, my family, and my future.

I lasted three days.

The holiday season was in full swing when the medical team arrived at my home. Interestingly enough, the doctor in charge of my detox put me on Suboxone. I would finally be properly utilizing this medicine after they were no longer paying me to endorse it. But even with Suboxone, the withdrawals were excruciating, and soon, my inner self began to whisper that this was too much. *Screw it,* the voices in my head told me. *You don't want to do this. You're in your own home. You can leave whenever you want.* A terrible case of the "fuck-its" infected my psyche, and I made the decision to bounce from detox.

Lauren and my family foresaw this outcome. To combat it, they had not only hidden all my car keys, but they'd even let the air out of some of the tires of my cars. Those preparations weren't enough to stop a determined Situation. I scoured the house, eventually finding my Lamborghini keys underneath a floor tile.

At the time, I had about seven luxury cars housed in a big barn garage at the back of the property. Lambo key in hand, I made a dash for the garage, which I found locked. As I searched for a way in, Yolanda, the large and extremely tough nurse assigned to my detox, tackled me from behind. Today, I think what she did was amazing, but at the time, I was like, *What the hell? What kind of service am I paying for?*

Yolanda and I hit the ground, and I rolled away like it was a "stop, drop, and roll" exercise. Escaping her clutches, I leapt up and dropkicked my own garage door, bashing it in until I made entry. As I opened the other garage door and hopped into the Lamborghini, a flash of movement crossed my peripheral. I heard a shout. Lauren and my brother Frank had run out of the house and were now in pursuit. Frank yelled,

"I'm calling the cops!" while Lauren made a dash for another one of my vehicles, a BMW M5. I peeled out, driving over my lawn to avoid hitting those whom I perceived as my captors and made my escape. In the rearview mirror, I saw the lights of the M5 flick on.

The chase was on. Lauren started out hot on my heels in the M5, but I got some separation and pulled into a QuickChek for some cash before heading to my drug dealer's house. By the time I ran out of the store, Lauren had caught up and was now blocking me in. She screamed that she was calling the cops, telling me, "This is crazy! You need to get back home!"

But I wasn't hearing it. I jumped back in the Lambo and, tires screeching, snuck around the M5 and accelerated back onto the main road. Lauren was quickly back in pursuit, but not before smacking the side of the M5 into a dumpster.

We raced through the South Jersey streets in these high-powered racecars in the direction of my plug's house. Suddenly, I saw a cop car in my rearview mirror. My heart sank. I felt terrible. I was deathly sick from withdrawals, with no shoes on, trying to escape my caring girlfriend, all while putting us in grave danger. It was a fiasco. Still, I wasn't ready to give up yet.

"Mike, what the hell's going on?" the cop asked me. "Why are you driving so erratically?"

"Sorry, officer, but there's a crazy fan following me. I was just trying to get away from her," I responded.

The cop looked back at Lauren in the M5. "Isn't that your car?" he asked.

I took a deep breath. I couldn't keep doing this. "Yeah, that's my girl," I admitted. "We're going home."

I realized I wasn't going to escape Lauren. She was too strong, too determined. She cared about me too much. She'd just lost her brother and didn't want to lose me too. This beautiful woman's personality had no quit. So I had to. I gave up. I went home and finished a torturous detox under Lauren's, Yolanda's, and Dr. Sam's watchful eyes.

The family show being a go may have given me a push to get off opiates and alcohol again, but because I wasn't getting sober for the right reasons, it really had no chance of sticking.

A familiar cycle commenced after the latest detox. Once more, I went on Vivitrol. But I also started right back on the steroids, adding them to a repertoire of even more Adderall, Valium, and weed. This steroid cycle was more intense than the previous one with the copious amount of tren I was injecting sending even more anger coursing through my brain and body. By the time filming rolled around for the family show, I was a mess. Incredibly paranoid and delusional. The voices in my head were worse. Looking back, I realize I was losing my mind.

Still, I made every attempt to keep appearances up. Physically, I looked great. All the steroids allowed me to get incredibly jacked. Since it's essentially speed, I used Adderall as a tool to work out even harder and burn fat. I don't know how much I was actually fooling my loved ones, but I certainly thought I was keeping all my issues secret.

After her brother's passing, I wanted to take care of Lauren as much as possible. To take away those stressors of everyday life. She moved in with me, and I completely supported her. I loved Lauren with all my heart and didn't want to see her hurt in any way. As much as I could, I wanted to take that pain away from her. It wasn't always possible, but I tried as hard as I knew how.

Likewise, I continued supporting my family. The new show would provide us all with a paycheck, which I desperately needed. Expenses had been running high, and the incoming money was not keeping up. I'd had to downsize recently, selling off some of my cars. I eventually used our money woes to convince Lauren I should go off the Vivitrol shot, since it cost around a thousand dollars a month. (Immediately after jumping off the shot, I snuck out to my drug dealer's house and bought a hundred pack of Blues.)

For the first time, I started worrying about money. The walls seemed to be crumbling around me. What last-ditch effort does a reality star lean on when he needs to super-inject his career and make a quick paycheck?

The same secret weapon that launched or reignited the careers of people like Kim K., Paris Hilton, and Tommy Lee: the sex tape.

I'd kept a "break glass in case of emergency" sex tape in a safe in my office for years, a last-resort insurance policy if I was ever desperate enough. Was this the time to cash that policy and release the tape? I huddled with my team, trying to decide if I was willing to cross this threshold. Keep in mind, this wasn't just any ordinary sex tape—this was a Situation sex tape, involving multiple participants, and it would have blown the world's mind.

"Listen, guys, I think it's time to break out the big guns," I said. Then, off my team's confused looks, I continued. "I've been saving a sex tape for a few years now, only to bring it out during an emergency. I think this is that emergency."

They didn't seem surprised. "Are you sure you want to do that?" Marc asked. "Once you cross this line, there's no turning back."

"I think now is the time." Everyone nodded their heads, and we all agreed not to divulge this secret operation to Lauren, Melissa, or my mom.

We did our due diligence by speaking with the lawyers and then started shopping the video to Vivid and the other big adult entertainment companies. At the end of the day, the offers we received were not attractive enough to go that route, so I ended up aborting mission. But it's funny to think how close the world came to having a public Situation sex tape.

I still needed money and wasn't sure what to do. *Should I invest what money I had left? Buy real estate?* I decided to start a business in a field I was an expert in—tanning. With my last $300,000, I opened a tanning salon in Middletown and hired my whole family to work there. I figured it would be great content for this new show while also providing a good living.

When the money for the family show finally hit the bank account, I remember shedding a tear of relief. I had bet on myself, as I always did, and it seemed like this would be another wager that paid off. Filming commenced with most of the storylines revolving around the Sorrentino family running my tanning salon. We were a hot-blooded, close-knit Italian family with big personalities, and the pressure cooker of running the tanning salon led to some memorable fights.

Boca Tanning Club began bringing in good monthly revenue, but the business wasn't profitable because of how much I was paying in salaries. Rapidly dwindling resources became an additional stressor on top of my addiction and tax issues, and I grew more and more paranoid. The best way to describe it is that I believed everyone was out to get me.

Frank was running the tanning salon for me, and I was unhappy with the job he was doing. One day, after he didn't pick up my call, I decided I'd had enough. I jumped into my new Ferrari 458—which I had stupidly purchased after cashing out an IRA and getting killed in taxes and penalties—and raced to the salon to confront him. I remember being super high on Adderall. Since going off Vivitrol, I'd recently started dabbling with Oxy again, and seven Roxys waited in my pocket for when I needed to come down later.

I came into the salon hot that day, 'roid rage and Adderall paranoia mixing in a dangerous amalgamation. My energy was aggressive to say the least. Right off the bat, Frank gave me attitude. *How dare he!* When he shrugged me off, I didn't appreciate the disrespect and followed him down the hall to the office, where he slammed the door in my face and locked it behind him. Not knowing my mother and sister were already in there, I stepped back and side-kicked the door, splintering it and inadvertently hitting all three of them. Frank and I began to wrestle and fight while Mama Peaches and Melissa shrieked and attempted to get us to stop. My mom jumped on my back to try to stop me from tearing Frank apart while Melissa called the cops. After they arrived and as the cuffs went on, I couldn't help but think, *How am I getting arrested in my own tanning salon right now? This is definitely going to be on TMZ.*

Down at the police station, the officers began processing me. They hadn't yet frisked me, and it occurred to me that if they did and discovered the seven Roxys in my pocket, I would catch drug charges as well. The only sensible solution I could come up with was to somehow consume the pills before they were discovered. So, surrounded by officers as I sat in my own cell the size of a standup tanning bed, in between answering the intake questions, I stealthily slipped my fingers into my pocket and gingerly removed a single pill. When the officer turned to his monitor to type in my answer, I slickly placed it under my tongue.

"Name?"

"Michael Paul Sorrentino."

He typed while I nonchalantly sucked on a pill.

"Date of birth?"

"July 4, 1981."

Another sour pill pushed through pursed lips. Then another. Eventually, I was able to choke all seven down with no water. By the end of the intake process, I was so high that even the TMZ cameras outside upon my release could not remove the smile from my face. A guilty plea leading to court-ordered anger management meant another narrow escape from serious charges.

The fight didn't slow down filming of *The Sorrentinos*. After shooting one of the final scenes in upstate New York, the cast and crew drove back to Jersey in a caravan. I was on so much Adderall that I hadn't slept at all the night before, and my mind was playing tricks on me. It's hard to describe, but I kept hearing and seeing things that weren't there. I was not operating in real life—it felt like I was in *The Matrix*. I was so paranoid that I had confiscated a forearm-sized steak knife from the set of the home we had filmed at in Coxsackie and placed it in my Louis Vuitton bag for protection. Protection from what or whom, I didn't know. I was out of my mind. A threat in the matrix, I guess. But in my head, I needed a weapon.

At some point during this casual drive south, I began to believe that everyone in the car was involved in some nefarious plot to get me—the crew, the producers, even Frank and Lauren, who were in the back seat. I decided I wasn't going down without a fight. At a toll booth, I made my move. With no warning, I jumped out of the car and ran over to the driver's side. I told the production assistant who was driving to get the fuck out of the car, kicking him out and commandeering the vehicle.

My paranoid, convoluted brain told me that I needed to take control of this situation.

Everyone in the car grew startled and uneasy as I aggressively jumped behind the wheel and led us back onto the highway. An awkward silence filled the van. Unfortunately, it was on brand for me to do something crazy, so no one seemed too alarmed at my behavior. Yet.

Soon, I was cruising along at 110 miles per hour in this production van, weaving in and out of traffic, trying to escape a nonexistent threat that I had determined was a van of Hasidic Jews we had previously passed. I had convinced myself they were actually hitmen. As I made my escape, I continued looking around wildly at everyone in the van and warning them that I knew what they were up to. I turned to Frank, threatening, "If anything is going on and I find out about it, you're the first one to get it." Then, I looked at my girlfriend. "Lauren, you get a pass."

Even though no one in the van had any idea what was going on, they were rightfully terrified. Clearly, I was capable of anything. Everyone sat quietly, unsure what to do as I pushed the limits of safety and the capabilities of the van's engine. Finally, Frank half-joked, "Anyone want a Valium?" Amidst nervous laughter, I think everyone took him up on his offer, including myself, thankfully. Eventually, the Valium calmed my nerves enough that I no longer believed the people who loved me had lined up to plot against me or that hitmen were following us.

As the ride continued and it became clear to me this was all in my head, I relaxed the grip on the knife, still in the bag on my lap. Tensions deflated. By the time I pulled into the driveway of my house in Manchester, safe and sound, everyone—sedated on Valium—looked at each other, silently communicating, *Oh my God, what just happened?* before going about the rest of their day.

The Sorrentinos didn't get renewed for a second season. As expenses ran out of control at the tanning salon, I had to close it. Lauren and I moved out of my large single-family home in Manchester and into a townhouse in Aberdeen. Frank and Pete, who had been living with us in the bigger house, decided to go out on their own.

Meanwhile, my legal issues from the tax case were ramping up. The government's investigation had been going on for years by now, and despite me burying my head in the sand and trying to ignore the inevitable, it wasn't going away. Aside from my wonderful, beautiful, understanding girlfriend, the only consistency in my life remained the drugs. Everything else had fallen apart.

Whether I wanted to admit it or not, the inevitable crash landing seemed imminent.

CHAPTER 22

ROCK BOTTOM

It was my regular morning routine whenever I was home: hit up the neighborhood bagel shop for my coffee, lemon Gatorade, and a bacon, egg, and cheese on everything bagel with salt, pepper, and ketchup. The ritual offered some much-needed normalcy—or least what passed for normalcy in my world. As the girl behind the counter finished taking my order, I told her to throw in a newspaper like Dad used to do. After grabbing my copy of the *New York Post*, I took my place among the throngs while we waited for our numbers to be called.

Of course, the second I walked in, everyone in the place had stopped what they were doing to look at me. I was used to that. Mine is a familiar face that, by that point, the public had been viewing regularly on TV for years. I didn't consider the phenomenon something negative, nor did I frown upon the notoriety. It was part of my job, a job that had presented me with untold benefits. Some difficulties as well, of course, but most of those were self-inflicted.

However, for some reason, this particular morning, the stares seemed a little more pointed. Almost judgmental. A non-famous person might have feared food on their face or maybe became worried their fly was down. I simply assumed it was a normal public appearance for The Situation. But when I looked down at the front page of the newspaper in my hands, I saw the real reason for their stares.

A giant color photograph of me, looking dapper in a blue Tom Ford suit, stared back. It had been taken the day before on the infamous court-house steps in Newark, where my brother Marc and I had pleaded not guilty to tax evasion charges. The headline screamed, "'The Situation' rejects plea deal over tax fraud charges."

While the investigation had slowed to a crawl over the past couple of years, the government had nothing but time and resources to make a case. It was foolish to have clung to this glimmer of hope that they

155

would ever cease their hunt and think that this would all just eventually go away on its own. Maybe (probably) due to my constant intoxication, I'd convinced myself that none of it was real. For so long, I'd managed to bury reality and ignore the facts slapping me across the face. I suppose in a sense I was delusional, the culmination of melting my brain with so many drugs for so many years. Some days, I thought I was in *The Hunger Games*.

The previous day's court appearance—and now the physical proof in newsprint—was finally the crystal-clear evidence I needed to convince myself this was real life. It wasn't a dream or even a nightmare. The government was coming after me and wanted to throw me in prison.

The realization didn't cause me to so much as flinch. I didn't hang my head, didn't get upset. As everyone in the bagel place stared at the indicted reality star they were reading about on Page Six, I came to terms with reality. The case was on, and I would have to fight to clear my name.

I folded the *Post* and stuck it under my arm. Upon further reflection, I also purchased a copy of *The Daily News*. Both featured my perp walk on their cover. I decided I would save these official records as mementos in case I ever got myself out of this mess.

Finally understanding the severity of my legal issues didn't fundamentally change much. I still had to fight the case and continue paying the lawyers. By this point, I was in for close to a million dollars in legal fees. I was bleeding money. Lauren and I had no choice but to continue belt-tightening. The luxury cars were long gone. We even had to sell designer bags and shoes for spare cash. Some endorsement money and residual checks from MTV were still coming in, but that barely paid the rent on our townhouse, let alone maintained the lifestyle we'd grown accustomed to. We couldn't afford to go out to eat. When a nice check landed from WE tv's *Marriage Boot Camp: Reality Stars*, on which Lauren and I appeared in May of 2015, the money went straight to the lawyers.

With my ongoing addiction and the acceleration of the case jointly weighing on me, depression and anxiety set in once again. In an effort to mask my emotions and fight the stress, I continued to self-medicate.

But my bail terms—which allowed both me and Marc to remain free on $250,000 bonds—required me to stay away from drugs and alcohol and submit to routine drug tests to prove it.

Well, as we know, I was never great with authority, and my mindset was, *This is ridiculous. This isn't a drug case. How can you tell me I can't drink or party while I'm waiting to prove my innocence on tax charges?*

I believed I had done nothing wrong, yet the courts wanted to tighten the clamp on me. I was not willing to give in. I didn't want to be told what to do. Call it the immovable force against the unstoppable object. I didn't stop using and began to fail the pretrial drug tests. I popped positive for weed, steroids, and opiates because—duh—I was smoking weed, doing steroids, and taking Oxy.

Of course, I had my excuses ready to go. I told the court that I had done steroids in the past, and though I was off them now, they would still be in my system for six months. Okay, that bought me a six-month buffer, but it didn't stop my steroid cycles. I then went to a doctor for OxyContin and Valium prescriptions so I could claim those chemicals in my system were legit. But the pretrial officers began counting my pills to see if I was abusing them, which, of course, I was. Fed up with my failed drug tests and general bullshit, they really started to crack down.

I got assigned the toughest pretrial officer they had. Lori was her name. Probably a grandmother, Lori was a seasoned drug and alcohol abuse specialist about to retire when they charged her with fixing my ass. Tough as nails and deficient of bullshit, Lori probably saved my life. Where I had previously been able to lie and make excuses for my behavior to everyone else in my life, Lori wasn't having it. She let me know if the failed drug tests continued, she'd put me in front of the judge and recommend I be remanded to jail until my trial. I knew she meant business. Still, it took one more major escalation to make me see the light.

I've never told this next story before. No one alive knows it happened. Not Laurens—my wife and the mother of my children now, my girlfriend at the time. Not my mom, previously unaware she probably saved my life that day. The only person who knew this story was my best friend from childhood, Chris, and only because he was there. But Chris wasn't as fortunate as me—he lost his battle with addiction a year or so after this happened, and the tale went with him to the grave. Until now.

I had run out of pills. My resources weren't what they used to be. I called Chris up and asked if he could get anything. He said he knew a guy in Newark. I was like, "Dude, man, I can't go to Newark. My face is all over the news. Everyone knows me."

"Bro, I'll just jump out of the car and grab it. We'll be in and out. No one will see you."

I knew I had no choice. Withdrawals would start soon. I also knew Lauren would kill me if she found out I was with Chris. She'd know exactly what we were doing. She had an intuition for this type of thing, and we got in a huge fight before I left. I told her, "Listen, I'm a grown man. I'm just going for a drive to blow off some steam." I stormed out and picked up Chris.

For the next several hours, we drove my very recognizable—at least in the state of New Jersey—white Corvette throughout the inner city in search of our drugs of choice: Roxicet or oxycodone or really any prescription opiates. The entire time, a bad feeling pulsated through my being. This wasn't me. I didn't go into the hood to score drugs. I always had enough money that I didn't have to do this, didn't have to put myself in jeopardy. But Chris did. This was his wheelhouse. I gave him the money and waited in the car.

In his fearlessness, Chris visited housing complex after housing complex while I languished in the passenger's seat, trying to remain inconspicuous as a cacophony of sirens reverberated constantly in the not-too-far distance. This was the wild, wild west, and soon enough, the locals began to notice me. The Situation. From *Jersey Shore*. Under federal indictment. *What the hell am I doing here?* Being seen on a drug hunt in the ghetto was not a good idea. Yet here I was.

Each time Chris came up short, I realized how exposed I was. After sweating in the car for hours, my heart beating a million miles a minute, I began to get frantic. Each strikeout felt like a dagger. All signs pointed to this being a horrible idea. Lauren was calling and texting over and over, irate, pretty sure I was getting high. I ignored her.

Chris tried one more connect. He swore this guy would come through. He must have been inside the high-rise for an hour. My anxiety was in overdrive. I was sure he'd been arrested or worse. Finally, Chris sauntered out like a hero returning from the battlefield. He bounced into the driver's seat with a confident grin and a pep in his step. "We're good," he said happily, throwing a package into my lap. *Success. Thank God.*

I unwrapped it hurriedly, ready to pop four or five Oxys into my mouth and feel that welcome wash of relief. To my surprise, it wasn't pills I found wrapped in the napkin. Instead, it was a wax bundle tied together with rubber bands. Carefully, I opened the package. Inside was a sandy yellowish powder. I'd never seen anything like this before.

"'The fuck is this?" I asked, hoping it wasn't what I thought it was but knowing full well it was.

"It's the same thing," Chris assured me nonchalantly.

I looked at him, my expression again screaming, *What the fuck!?* "What do you mean it's the same thing?" My voice transmitted my fears: "This better not be what I think it is."

But it was. It was heroin. I was devastated. Not only because Chris had come up empty on his mission to find pills but because, deep down, I must have realized I was going to do it. I'd never done heroin before, unlike so many others who had found themselves addicted to pain pills and made that leap. I'd always sworn to myself that I would never fall that far. Not me. I was a TV star. I had money. I was famous. I drew the line at pills. But now, desperate, I knew I was probably going to cross that line. I felt powerless. I was going to try heroin.

I dropped Chris off and went home, the bundle buried secretively in my pocket. Lauren was furious at my disappearing act. She asked to see my phone. When she saw Chris's name, she knew where I'd been, what I'd been doing. "Oh my God, you were getting high!" she screamed in despair before slamming the door.

I went upstairs. I took out the bundle. As of yet, I still hadn't tried it. This was the moment of truth. Would I go down this path?

I sat in the bedroom, contemplating. I harbored no illusions. I was staring down the point of no return. If I accepted this escalation, would

I ever be able to come back? I knew most didn't. I also knew that soon withdrawals would begin to ravage my body and mind, and the grainy, sandy substance in my hands would prevent that. Besides, could my life get any worse? I was depressed, broke, strung out, facing prison, and the relationship with the love of my life was hanging on by a thread.

Fuck it, I finally thought, opening the bundle. I accepted this was Russian roulette. Not wanting to OD, I decided to try just a little bit, to dip my toe. I removed the rubber band. Took out my keys. Dipped the corner of one into the powder. Carefully brought it to my face. And snorted just the tiniest bit of heroin to see what would happen. I waited, half-expecting it to kill me. But it wasn't much. I didn't get the rush or euphoria I was expecting.

My first thought was, *Oh my God, I don't like it. I don't like it!* I was elated with the reaction. I knew so many people like Chris; once they got their first taste of heroin, it was all over. I didn't like the feeling—did that mean I could avoid that outcome?

I considered flushing the rest down the toilet. The bump I'd done made me slightly high, at least taking the edge off, but I felt dirty. Then, another thought came into my head. *Why don't I try a little more? Maybe it will intensify the effect.*

At that exact moment, as I was deciding, my phone rang. It was my mom.

"Hello?"

"Michael? Is everything okay?"

I had the bundle in the palm of my hand. I put it down. "Yeah, Ma, I'm fine. Why? What's up?"

"I just had a bad feeling that something was wrong. Are you really okay?"

I was like, *Oh my God, am I in* The Truman Show *right now?* I literally looked around the room for hidden cameras. How had she known that I was in grave danger? It was a come-to-Jesus moment. My mom's call had stopped me from doing more heroin. Had that happened, who knows where I would be today. It was a crazy and unbelievable occurrence that I immediately saw as nothing less than a sign from God. At the same time, Lauren began knocking at the door. It was that exact moment that I finally gave up. I surrendered. I would do whatever it took to find lasting sobriety.

I collected myself as best I could, then told my mom I was fine, that I loved her, and that I was going to bed. I hung up and went into the bathroom, and as Lauren continued knocking, I flushed the heroin. I watched as the bindle spun around the bowl, sinking, until finally, it was gone. I couldn't help but feel like it was the first step in a new, long journey.

I was proud of what I had done. Proud I had stood on the precipice and managed to not fall in. A sense of beginning washed over me.

I opened the door and let Lauren in. I was emotional. She was emotional, even though she had no idea I had just snorted heroin. (Still doesn't...until she reads this.) Tears streamed down both our faces.

"I'm sorry, baby. I don't want to fight," she said, taking me by the hands.

I kissed her. I hugged her. I squeezed her tight against my shaking body. "I don't want to fight either. I love you," I said. "I'm done. I'm sick and tired of being sick and tired. I'm going to get the help I need."

After I wiped the tears from my love's face, I picked up the phone. Even though it was after hours, I dialed Lori, my pretrial officer, and left a message that it was important I talk to her. She called back almost immediately. I told her I surrendered. I was waving the white flag. I admitted that I had a problem and needed to go to rehab. She said she was proud of me, that she applauded me for my strength and courage. We reflected on what a big moment this was, and then Lori instructed me to check in at Discovery Institute in Marlboro, New Jersey, in the morning.

It would be the first day of the rest of my life.

CHAPTER 23

SURRENDER AND THE FINAL REHAB

Money, like water, flows in only one direction. Sometimes, that direction can change suddenly and without warning. For me, the current had turned 180 degrees; instead of revenue coming in faster than I could spend it, as it had for years, money was now gushing in the opposite direction—out. I was flat broke. Worse—I was in major debt.

I already explained how Lauren and I had downsized as much as humanly possible. We now shared a car, a Toyota Camry, after the white Corvette was repossessed. The rent on our modest townhouse in Aberdeen was only $2,700 a month, but we were behind on it and being threatened with eviction. There were no more Louis Vuitton bags or Manolo Blahnik shoes to sell.

My attempts at doing the things I thought I needed to do to dig us out of this mess seemed to be too little, too late. I'd hired new accountants and management, but it didn't seem to be helping the grim financial predicament. By the time I decided to go back to rehab, I was broke and about to be homeless. Nearly every dollar that came in went to the mountain of lawyer bills I was drowning under. My company had been paying the legal bills for both Marc and myself, but by this point in the case, I could afford neither. As the trial date approached, I was no longer able to even pay my own attorney and had to let him go. If there ever were dire straits, this was it.

The morning after trying heroin, Lauren called my family and explained that I was on my way back to rehab. I'm sure there was some eye-rolling and disbelief on their part, rightfully so. They'd seen this before, too many times. Of course they were skeptical, doubtful I could ever get my life back on track. Honestly, I shared their doubts. It was my fourth attempt at getting clean, and I think we all had started to lose a little bit of hope.

To my father's credit, while I checked into the facility Lori had set up for me, he helped Lauren pack up our belongings and place them in storage. We weren't even sure we could afford the $400-a-month fee for the unit. How far the mighty had fallen.

Lauren moved back in with her parents and got a job at Lululemon. We had no idea what the future held. She contemplated graduate school. As I began what I had resolved to make my final stint in rehab, I thought hard about the choices that had landed me here. I'd worked so hard to make all my dreams come true. I'd been on top of the world. Money, fame, a woman who loved me. And through my own bad decisions and weaknesses, I'd let it all slip through my fingers. I was beyond disappointed in myself. I'd lost everything. I was completely destroyed. This time, I was finally broken. Maybe that was exactly what I needed.

It had taken me years and years of rash behavior almost costing me my life to reach this dark place. I knew there would be no more chances. I had to man up. Deep in the darkness, with no one to blame but myself for this predicament, I asked what would happen if I really applied myself and put everything I had into getting sober. Could I reach the top of the mountain once again?

I knew that for there to be any hope of finding lasting sobriety, I would have to approach recovery differently from my previous attempts. It was imperative I get out of my own way and put forth every ounce of effort I possessed in what I recognized would need to be a heroic attempt to conquer this disease once and for all. It was now or never. There were no fifth chances.

I had bad credit. The government was coming after me for millions of dollars I no longer possessed. My steadiest employer, MTV, had lost faith in me. Other networks had lost faith in me. My family had lost faith in me. Even my girlfriend had probably lost some faith in me, and I wasn't sure how much longer I could count on her standing by my side if I didn't get my life together. What I couldn't do was lose faith in myself. I *had* to succeed in staying sober this time. What's the definition of insanity? Doing the same thing over and over and expecting different results. This time, I was determined to do it their way.

You see, I finally realized what the problem was: me. I had an obsessive personality, and nothing was going to change that. But what if I embraced that character trait and used it for good? I realized the only way I would find success was if I could harness and redirect that obsessiveness to feed myself only positive behaviors.

The easiest way to explain it is that we all have a good wolf and a bad wolf inside us. The wolf you feed always wins. For years, I'd only fed the bad wolf—ego, money, drugs, sex, material items. When you do bad, you get bad. I had to reverse that and only feed myself positive behaviors and mindsets. Slowly, over time, I began to remove anything negative from my life in an attempt to only feed the good wolf.

I created a list in my head. Anything unconstructive got eliminated. I stayed away from the people, places, and things that didn't align with where I wanted my life to go. I knew these corrections wouldn't happen all at once, but by making small changes one day at a time, one week at a time, one month at a time, I began to remove those negative influences and distance myself from problems, drama, and temptation.

I remember sitting in my shared room in the rebab center shortly after intake. I was miserable. I didn't want to be there. I was going through withdrawals. Those familiar burdens—anxiety, depression, and self-doubt—were at a ten. I didn't like the food. I didn't like the people. I didn't necessarily like the counselors. But I also knew that I didn't want to be in a place like this ever again. If this was going to be the last time, I had to give it my all. No more trying to do it Mike's way. I needed to completely surrender and do whatever the professionals suggested. The therapists, the doctors, the counselors, and those in recovery who had come before me and been successful—I had to trust them absolutely and adhere totally to their advice and guidance.

So that's what I did. I completely surrendered and submitted to the program. For the first time, I was a model patient. I put all my energy into getting clean. I went to all the sessions, did all the work. Followed the twelve steps. I shared during group and gave it my all in every aspect of the program. I was honest, accountable, and truthful in this attempt to reverse the failures of my past. For the first month of that stint in rehab, I did everything right. Then came Christmas Eve 2015.

As you can tell from the opening of this book, Christmas holds a special place in my heart. It's a cherished time to be spent with family and those you love. Instead, I was here in this place with these people. The drugs had left my body, leaving me to deal once again with years of suppressed trauma. I was sad and depressed and in a vulnerable state. I missed my family and girlfriend.

Another patient had smuggled in Roxys and asked if I wanted one. In a moment of weakness and desperation, I took it. I immediately regretted the decision, but it was too late. I was now high in rehab and felt terrible about this sudden relapse. Worse, someone ratted us out, and the next thing I knew, the government was informed about my slipup. There was talk of kicking me out of rehab and potentially sending me to jail. But in the end, Lori understood that relapses are a part of recovery and generously gave me another chance—a chance I took seriously, knowing it would be my last.

I did an extra forty-five days in the facility after the slipup and can proudly say that day at the end of 2015 was the last time I ever used.

After completing more than two months of inpatient rehab, it was suggested I attend an intensive outpatient program for another six months. Finally ready and determined to get out of my own way and take the advice of the professionals and others who had been successful in the program, I happily obliged. After completing that program, I then did an additional two months of one-on-one therapy with one of the therapists from Discovery. In total, with the slipup, I did nearly a year of treatment. But the work wasn't over. I acknowledge it never will be.

Though I had no interest in getting a sponsor, it was advised that I do so. Immediately, I began searching for the right one. I found a guy who was rough around the edges like I was whom I thought I could relate to. Then, the professionals advised me to create a recovery network, so I did that as well. They said to attend ninety meetings in ninety days—Alcoholics Anonymous, Narcotics Anonymous, it didn't matter. I not only attended, I participated. I worked the program. Basically, anything they suggested I do that would move me closer to achieving lasting sobriety, I did. And more. Exercise and diet again became an important part of my life. I started to dive deeper into my faith and God and my purpose in life. I continually told myself, *No matter how hard it gets, I will make it.*

This new philosophy was in direct contrast to how I'd gone about rehab in the past. Being successful in long-term sobriety requires more than treating only the physical aspects of addiction. I'd always merely detoxed my body from chemicals. That was the easy part. I also needed to focus on the mental and spiritual aspects of healing. I had to educate myself and grow from all the work I was putting in—taking my sobriety one day at a time, learning about myself, and taking total accountability for every decision in my life.

Understanding this was incredibly empowering. Life is a product of every one of our decisions, and if I was going to change my life, I had to start making the right choices. They say nothing changes if nothing changes, and I changed everything. I became obsessed with bettering myself. Any day I could execute change and eliminate negativity was considered a win. It took years to correct so many long-standing bad habits and behaviors. It was and still is a constant struggle. But it started with understanding these concepts, then implementing them.

One tool I learned in rehab was to "run the tape." Essentially, it's a risk assessment tool to analyze potential outcomes of a decision. Let's say you decide to drink and drive. "Run the tape" on possible consequences: You could get arrested. You could kill someone. You could kill yourself. These are all possible outcomes of making the wrong decision. I began applying this method to my decision-making process in just about every aspect of my life, to every conversation and interaction I had. Should I get into an argument with someone? What are the possible outcomes if I do? The answer is usually, "no, I shouldn't."

The anger management tools I learned in rehab were instrumental in changing how I operated. Think before you speak. If you are upset or emotional, cool off and walk away. Never let your emotions rule your intelligence. Get outside your body and try to understand what is happening. Understand the bigger picture of things. Get back to your standard operating procedure. Be grateful for today. Be grateful for the simple things like your job and family, food in the fridge, and your health. If you come from a default of positive energy, you attract more blessings and abundance. These are some of the things I learned and still wholeheartedly believe in.

But more than any other philosophy honed in rehab, I can say that buying into and living by the twelve steps was the most important. I felt like once I started working the steps, I was on the right road but in no rush to find the end of it. They call it aggressive patience. I took my time to complete each step because it was more about the journey than the destination. Recovery is a lifelong pursuit, so I focused on being mindful, simply happy to put one foot in front of the other.

I was also broken down enough by that point to finally accept and absorb the Serenity Prayer: "God grant me the serenity to accept the things I cannot change, the courage to change the things I can, and the wisdom to know the difference." I found those words extremely powerful. Adhering to and living by these core tenants of recovery changed my life.

After finally getting clean, I maintained the same schedule each and every day for a year and a half. Self-care has always been my foundation, and this routine gave me an important sense of structure and peace knowing I was on the right path. It was a new twist on an old regimen. Instead of GTL, it was GTM: gym, tan, meeting. Gym for my body, tanning because it made me feel and look good, and an AA or NA meeting to be around like-minded people. I wanted to hear their stories. I wanted to "get the hope," as they called it. These fellow addicts had been in similar, dark situations and had worked hard to pull themselves out of them. I tried to use their experiences—both successes and failures—as hacks for my own sobriety. Their tales were inspiring. It showed that people can and do beat this monster.

Recovery can be a daunting proposition. Success sometimes feels impossible and out of reach. The odds certainly didn't favor my lasting sobriety. With so many things working against me, it was nice to share those obstacles with people experiencing the same hardships. Seeing their blueprint made the possibility of sobriety seem realistic.

I continued concentrating on putting together Ws, baby steps that led to a string of good days. Then some more. Small victories. It wasn't easy, and it wasn't fast. But after practicing this method religiously, I found that I was happy for the first time in a long time. I enjoyed having a break from such a crazy lifestyle. I enjoyed not being weighed down by the cars, money, responsibilities, and stress. And I certainly enjoyed no longer being beholden to intoxicating substances.

I was simply happy to live a normal life. I didn't want to be seen. I only wanted to take care of myself. I wanted to be a good person. If someone was on the side of the road with a flat tire, I wanted to be the one to stop and help them change it. This was a rebuilding process, a master plan to create a new and improved Situation. If I did things right, I could use rock bottom as a trampoline to find my true self and purpose in life.

It would take years to undo the wreckage of my past, but I was on my way. I felt like I now had the secret recipe for success. If I could conquer addiction, then I could conquer anything. I became my own superhero, saving myself while inadvertently saving others by sharing my story.

That's why I wrote this book. If those suffering from addiction can hear how far I fell and how many times I failed before getting it right, I believe my story can give them hope and the confidence needed to find their own lasting sobriety. It's a beautiful gift to be able to save a life.

Recovery became my passion. It still is. I used my obsessive personality to get and stay clean. My sobriety came first in everything I did. As long as I kept that in the forefront of my mind, everything else would be a breeze. My new drug of choice was growth. All energy went into being my best self. I was determined to complete a legendary comeback—The Situation was morphing into The Inspiration.

Somewhere along the way, I found that I had become a good person. I led with kindness and was good to others. I made good decisions. I no longer lied, cheated, or stole. I didn't drink or drug. I didn't even drive fast because I couldn't afford the ticket. I continued doing positive things and maintaining positive habits and behaviors. Over time, I felt like I was distancing myself from the negativity.

Slowly, life got better. I figured that if I could keep turning one great day into two and eventually a month into a year, I could put together something beautiful. Something great, actually. If I could seize every day, I might just have a shot at that comeback.

It was a long road that I'm still traversing. I suspect I was living with a mental illness from all the speed (Adderall). It took a long time to get my brain healthy again. If I had gone to a doctor, I'm sure they would have prescribed heavy-duty meds under the guise of healing. But I didn't want any more chemical solutions. Instead, I leaned on exercise, healthy eating, and nature to get back to my baseline. Meetings and the twelve steps were my medicine.

Eventually, I found the peace that I had been seeking for so long. A peace that money can't buy, found only by living healthy and doing the right thing. My confidence was back, and people started wanting to be around me again. The phone began to ring. My family believed in me again. Lauren believed in me.

I rid myself of my last bad habit—smoking cigarettes. I was in good shape, though not six-pack shape. That was okay. I was more focused on laying a firm foundation of recovery than on my physique. I looked healthy.

Lori, my pretrial officer, raved about me when I'd previously been her worst pupil. I used to loathe getting called in for pee tests. I complained they were a violation of my rights, but really, it was because I knew I was going to fail them. Now, I was happy when they gave me drug tests; I knew they would validate the new man I was becoming.

Though still a work in progress, I certainly was on the right track. I was finding success beating something that most people die from. I felt very lucky. I felt grateful. I had found myself again and was slowly getting back to who I was supposed to be in life.

Earlier, Lauren and I had moved in with Frank, but it wasn't a good situation. We wanted our own place, so in 2016, when Food Network offered me a spot on their show *Worst Cooks in America: Celebrity Edition*,

I saw the income as a way for us to move out and get our own place. Still, I was hesitant to take the job. I didn't know if I wanted to be on TV again. I was still trying to find myself. I didn't want to get back into the old routine. I worried it could affect my sobriety.

I also wasn't sure whether I was still comfortable in front of the camera. Did I still have the same spark? The "it" factor? Did I still have the confidence and charisma America had fallen in love with? I was a different person now. Would The Situation be as interesting and entertaining sober? Honestly, I didn't know.

In the end, I decided to do the show. I always want to grow and challenge myself and not shrink away from something even if I'm uncomfortable doing it. I didn't know how or even if I could get it done, but I sure was going to do everything in my power to make the show a success.

Fortunately, it went great. I did a full season, ten episodes (shot over ten days or so), and was paid well. Lauren and I could get our fresh start. We rented a cute little two-bedroom apartment in Long Branch, right near the beach. We wanted to be on the water, near nature where the good energy is. It was a great place for me, Lauren, and our golden retriever, Moses, to establish some roots and enjoy the little things in life. It felt like home.

For me, it's always been about going to the shore. Back to my roots, where it all began. That's where we would start this next chapter of our life. With me sober, happy, and at peace.

Finally.

CHAPTER 24

KARMA RETURNED

I found that I was good at sobriety. I discovered I enjoyed the test and thrived on taking on challenges and not giving up. There was a realization that my purpose in life was to stay clean and sober, not only for myself but also for others looking to me for inspiration.

I maintained that if I could be successful at recovery, I could be successful at anything. It was far and away the most difficult thing I had ever attempted, let alone completed. This wasn't a part-time job. I had to work hard at recovery all day, every day.

My life had stabilized. Doing the *Worst Cooks in America* show and a subsequent family boot camp show on WE tv with my brothers paid the rent. Lauren and I no longer lived a life of abundance, but it was enough. We lived simply and smartly, enjoying each other and our new uncomplicated life. I was a good son, brother, partner, and human. I opened the door for others. I smiled at them. People wanted to be around me again. I continued working to remove negativity from my life while leaning on my faith.

As I write this, thinking about my transformation, I can't help but get emotional. I know how stacked the odds were against me and that it required throwing a perfect game to recover. So much could have gone wrong, and for so many dealing with addiction, it does. I'm proud that I was able to get through it and never turn back or give up. Nothing is stronger than a broken man rebuilding himself, and sobriety became my superpower.

Me and Lauren's relationship grew stronger as my sobriety did. We continued to be each other's rocks and anchors. The next year or so went by peaceably. I remained content with this simplistic life. I had a roof over my head. The bills were paid. I was mentally, physically, and spiritually healthy, working each and every day to continue growing into a better version of myself. The trappings that came with reality stardom had vanished, and I relished my new life. Lauren and I were perfectly happy in our two-bedroom condo, driving the Camry, living a quiet, sober existence. Things were smooth; things were easy. We didn't press. Whatever was going to happen would happen. Of course, the indictment hung over our heads as it slowly worked through the legal system, but I didn't let it get me down. I knew that too would turn out however it was supposed to.

Though it wasn't why I did it, the good energy I was putting out to the world seemed to come back twofold. The phone was ringing again. After the boot camp show, WE tv came back to us and said they wanted to reboot the family show, *The Sorrentinos*. My reps completed negotiations to get the show green-lighted, but then, at the last minute, just before the contracts were finalized, the network backed out. To this day, I can't say for sure why, but the news rolled off my back. My response was merely, "Okay."

I was of the belief that when God closes a door, he opens a window. Losing the show was fine with me. That wouldn't have been the case in the past. I probably would have argued with my team, blaming them, then gotten high and made more bad decisions. But the new Mike, filled with an inner harmony, had developed a healthier outlook. Basically, my feeling was, "If you don't want to work with me, that's fine. No hard feelings. Something else will come along." I didn't get angry, didn't dwell on it. Just kept it moving. I knew with sobriety on my side, I couldn't be stopped.

I hadn't communicated with any of my *Jersey Shore* castmates in years while I focused on my health. From afar, I'd watched all the great things they were doing, rooting them on and wishing the best for each of them. They were doing their thing while I concentrated on recovery. But I saw them working, starting families, living their best lives. And even though we didn't interact, I always felt like we would run into each other again someday. The spark we had ignited so many years before had inspired a generation and culture; that magic was a once-in-a-lifetime thing. A bond like that could never be broken. I assumed when the time was right, something would happen between us again. We had been so young when the show ended; even all these years later, it felt like we had unfinished business.

In 2017, the phone rang again. Burger King wanted to shoot a mini *Jersey Shore* reunion with the whole cast. They were introducing a chicken parmesan sandwich, and who better to promote it than the OG guidos and guidettes? Pauly, Vinny, Jenni, Sammi, Nicole, Deena, and I all quickly accepted.

The opportunity felt like a sign from the universe. All my positive vibes being emitted into the ether were being redirected toward me. I was excited to get back with the squad and felt something big would come from it. History would definitely repeat itself—I just knew it. This may have been an extended commercial for a fast-food joint, but I was confident putting the seven of us back in a room together in front of cameras would rekindle that magic we had imparted to the public years earlier. Overall, I was just happy and grateful for the chance. I was a proponent of "if you deserve it, the universe is going to serve it" and felt like this was good karma being returned.

Still, there were definitely some nerves associated with seeing my castmates again. The last time we had all been together, I'd still been struggling with addiction. I probably wasn't a very good person back then. They didn't know the new Mike. Would they even be willing to give him a chance?

I couldn't wait to show them how much I'd changed. By this point, I had almost two years of sobriety under my belt. I was a different man than they had known. I was proud of who I'd become—sober, positive, thriving in a committed relationship. Someone who—despite the adversity of my marathon tax evasion case—was enjoying a calm within the storm. I was eager for them to see that, to meet the new Mike.

I certainly wasn't the same Situation, though that moniker will always be a part of my identity. But I found I had slowly developed an updated identity from working my ass off in this never-ending attempt to grow into the ultimate version of myself. Someone honorable whom my friends and family could be proud of. I called this new iteration "Big

Daddy Sitch," or BDS. Just like The Situation character, BDS was a creative and authentic version of who I was at the time. I relied upon the same formula to create BDS as I had used for The Situation. Big Daddy Sitch was a genuine and (hopefully) entertaining version of the man who preferred chicken tendies to OxyContin and was in a committed, monogamous relationship.

That meant showing the world my vulnerable side. I could tell no lies. I would have to reveal my truth and be honest about my failings. Who I now was and who I had been previously would all be on display. I may no longer have had a six-pack, but I was still funny as fuck. And I had an amazing journey to share with my castmates and the world. It would take a leap of faith, but I had to be true to myself and hope that the world would be as enamored with BDS as they had been with The Situation.

Any doubts I had about reconnecting with my castmates melted away immediately upon walking into that Burger King. It was as if no time had passed. Like seeing a brother or sister for the first time in years. Everybody was so happy to be together again. There were hugs and laughs and jokes and all positive vibes. It felt like a catch-up dinner with family, because really, that's what it was.

But it was also work for us. It was a job, an opportunity to make some money. And the work was still very good. We were on point—funny, charismatic, and entertaining. The energy and atmosphere present during the filming of that Burger King commercial proved that our connection was still very much intact. That lightning in a bottle we'd captured so many years before had not escaped.

We all left feeling like we wanted more. A group chat started, and we wondered why we had ever stopped doing the show. It felt like we were picking up right where we had left off.

A few months later, Lauren and I attended Deena's wedding, along with everyone else aside from Ronnie. This happy event offered a big opportunity to repair the relationships with my castmates. The old Situation would have probably shown up drunk or high or maybe not shown up at all. But they teach you in recovery to show up for your friends, so that's what I did.

The crew recognized my efforts. They witnessed the difference. This wasn't filming for a few hours. This was a party with an open bar, and I was a different person than they had known. They were taking shots and having a great time. I was not taking shots and having a great time too. They could tell I was doing the right thing. They were super impressed, and I think it made a big impact on them. *Holy shit—Mike really is sober. He's a different man.*

Something else I learned in recovery was the phrase "by attraction, not promotion." Actions speak louder than words. I need to show you, not tell you. I wasn't asking anyone to be my friend or encouraging them to be around me. They *wanted* to be around me because they saw I was a good person. I showed it with love. By doing the right thing over and over and being my best self. They could see it in my eyes, in my presence. It wasn't easy, but by then, I'd been doing it for years. They could tell by my aura and energy. The lines of communication and friendship had reopened. It felt great to be back.

After a few months of continuing to do good, the next good thing happened. We'd been hearing whispers that MTV felt a certain way upon seeing the squad reunite and shoot a reunion on E! after the Burger King commercial was so well-received. Rumors of a *Jersey Shore* reboot abounded. The next phone call confirmed it: MTV was ready to start negotiations. Once the contracts were taken care of, they wanted to film season one in Miami.

The news was exhilarating but carried with it a certain amount of trepidation. I had major insecurities. This wasn't just a one-off reunion. This was a whole season of reality TV, living in a house with people drinking and partying. I was like, *Oh my God, I'm going back to the* Jersey Shore *days. Can I handle that? Am I going to succumb to that peer pressure, or am I going to be strong and continue my path forward in sobriety?*

I also still harbored those earlier concerns about how entertaining I would be clean and sober and whether I could still contribute to a hit show. This wasn't a commercial or a single episode—it was fourteen episodes with storylines that I would have to help carry. Could this new version of The Situation still do it? Would Big Daddy Sitch be as loved by the world as The Situation had been?

At the end of the day, I knew I had to do it. For myself, for my family, and for our future. The reality is I needed the job. I needed money. The tax case was coming to a head, and I had to pay for lawyers.

Besides, I wasn't one to back down from a challenge. It was an easy decision to take the leap of faith and do the show. *Jersey Shore* was back.

And so was The Situation.

CHAPTER 25

GUILTY

This *Jersey Shore* reboot felt like a second chance. An opportunity to do it right. If I could rise to the occasion, I just might be able to survive. I could make a life for my family. *If* I was successful. *If* I could stay sober. There were a lot of "ifs." I had no illusions as to how difficult it was going to be.

But I figured that if I could keep being my best self, taking it one day at a time, then nothing could stop me. That was my attitude—*don't get ahead of yourself. Just keep putting together those small Ws and doing the right thing each and every day.* As long as I did that, I knew something beautiful would happen.

As negotiations with MTV concluded (I settled for roughly $40,000 an episode for the reboot, less than a quarter of what I got during the heyday of *Jersey Shore* but more than enough for me and Lauren's uncomplicated lifestyle), my court case also seemed to be reaching a crescendo. The United States Government v. The Situation (the legal papers actually had "The Situation" on them) had been an ongoing battle with years of investigations, added and dropped charges, lawyer changes, and courtroom delays. I had no idea what the end result would be, but I knew that whatever happened, I would handle it with dignity and grace.

As the trial loomed closer, I repeated a prayer daily and lived by two phrases: "What was meant for my harm, God will turn for my good," and "No weapon formed against me shall prosper." I used these sayings as a tool, helping me to turn adversity into an advantage. I was ready for whatever was to come.

That simple but effective mindset meant positive vibes only as I prepared to travel to Miami and film the first episode of *Jersey Shore: Family Vacation* with the rest of the cast. I was excited. Lauren was excited. We recognized this as a huge opportunity to get my career back on track. I had worked so hard to manifest this second chance, and I was determined to seize the moment. You know the saying—I hadn't come this far just to come this far. In my head, the comeback wouldn't be complete until I was back on top of reality television. Recapturing the *Jersey Shore* magic with my roommates would most assuredly land me back on that revered perch.

At the same time, my court case had a major update. For years now, my lawyers had gone back and forth with the government. The prosecutors had offered various plea agreements, which carried different risks for jail time. I'd turned them all down. Rumors suggested that I was facing anywhere from five to fifteen years. I scoffed at those numbers. That sounded ridiculous to me. For what? Not knowing what was going on with my money? Not understanding banking laws?

In 2015, my accountant had pled guilty for evading taxes when filing my returns. I had no idea what he had done, and the government certainly had no evidence I'd had anything to do with whatever it was. No emails, text messages, or anything else from me. For a simple reason: I hadn't known what was going on with my finances.

During that time period—both when the alleged tax evasion occurred and during the onslaught of the case—I was high and mostly unaware of what was going on around me. I wasn't involved in the business aspect of The Situation. When my lawyers and accountants later audited my finances, they estimated I had spent a staggering $500,000 on drugs, mostly cocaine and oxycodone, during those years. Most people would have probably thrown themselves off a bridge after hearing that, but I kind of chuckled and shrugged my shoulders. Sounded about right. At the time, I didn't keep track of the money coming in. It may be a simple and dumb excuse, but it's the truth. I was so busy making the money, traveling, and fighting my addiction that if something had been done wrong with the taxes at the business, I didn't know about it and certainly hadn't been the one to do it. I simply wasn't paying attention.

I recognize how crazy it sounds that the leader of this multimillion-dollar corporation was nonexistent in his own business affairs. But that's the way the business was structured. I didn't do the books. I had accountants. I had a CEO, I had a CFO, I had a secretary. They were there to insulate me from those tasks.

That being said, I understand everything that happened was completely my fault. I may have thought I had checks and balances built into the business, but if I wasn't checking and balancing, then what good were they? My intoxication and lack of attentiveness meant things were destined to go awry. The buck stopped here with me.

But at the time, I looked at it like I was the talent. My job was to show up, smile, say something witty, and show my abs. I assumed my people had the rest taken care of. Guilty of ignorance, sure. But I didn't think much else. Certainly not knowingly participating in a conspiracy to defraud the American taxpayer like they were accusing me of doing. So I was reluctant to seriously consider a plea that meant guaranteed jail time, especially since I was a first-time offender.

The government tried another tactic, which to me was blasphemy. They wanted me to rat on my brother. To point the finger at Marc and say it had all been him in exchange for a reduced sentence. Hell no. I'm Italian. You never rat. You take care of your own. After that, I knew I had to take this to the end of the line. They were going to put me through hell, but if I could get through it, I knew I'd be stronger on the other side. And have a hell of a story to tell.

Now, finally sober, with a clear mind, I was able to objectively look at the case and listen to my lawyers. For the first time, I really examined what was going on. I was curious about what evidence the government had against me. It didn't seem like much. The prosecutors simply painted a picture of my lifestyle, which obviously wasn't proof of a tax crime.

As the trial date got closer, the government continued dangling a plea agreement that carried a risk of three years in prison in front of me. I was in such a good headspace at the time that I wasn't worried. I figured what was meant to happen would happen. I turned the offer down, deciding I'd risk trial. And needless to say, I wasn't going to turn on Marc.

I remember once the decision to go to trial had been made, Marc got super upset with me. He had already taken his plea deal and was worried that if I went to trial, I would lose. If that happened, I could be sent away for a long time. He was terrified for me.

Before trial, the prosecutors added charges in a superseding indictment. Remember that bag I carried to hold the cash from appearances? Well, upon returning from one high as balls, I took it to the bank in the interest of parking the cash somewhere safe. When I placed the money on the counter to deposit it, the teller handed me a form to fill out. In my state of mind, I wasn't too keen on completing any forms, so when she told me I could skip it if the amount deposited was under ten grand, I happily obliged and put part of the money back in the bag.

"Cool," I said. "Here's nine grand. I can come back and deposit the rest later."

The government used that as evidence I was avoiding reporting the cash. They even deposed that bank teller. But there was no ill intent there. I simply was high and paranoid and didn't want to waste time filling out the forms. (Because of this incident, I haven't stepped foot inside a physical bank for years. PTSD, I guess.)

At the conclusion of that superseding indictment hearing, Marc and I walked down a Newark street near the courthouse, not far from where Chris had scored the heroin right before I got clean. Marc's pleading eyes started to well up as he implored me to take the deal.

"Mike, they're not playing around. This isn't a game anymore. They are going to make an example out of you and put you away for a long time. You can't go to trial."

But I remained confident and undisturbed. The prosecutors were offering me a plea that would put me at an offense level of twelve. The sentencing guidelines in that category recommended prison time and not probation. I wasn't down with that. If they improved the offer to a level eleven, where probation was recommended, only then would I consider changing my plea. Unless that happened, I was determined to defend myself at trial.

I remained even-keeled and calm during the conversation, while Marc appeared panicked and frantic. He thought I didn't understand the danger I was in, and he was probably right. If I went to trial and lost, I would be facing jail time for all of the things my accountant had done wrong at the business, even though I was not part of it. I could end up in prison for years. He told me I was emotionless and ignoring reality. Again, there may have been some truth to his concerns. I even questioned myself in the moment. *Why aren't I more nervous and stressed about this?* But God had given me this inner peace, and there was an uncanny sense that no matter what happened, it was going to be okay. Whatever was coming, I had what it took inside to handle it.

"I know, Marc. We'll figure it out. Don't worry," I responded and walked away.

I rejected the government's plea deal. I rejected their offer to rat. Instead, I was focused and ready to defend myself at trial.

Then, weeks before the trial was set to begin, as I got ready to travel to Miami to film the *Jersey Shore* reboot, my phone rang. It was my attorney.

"You're not going to believe this," he said. I could hear the excitement in his voice.

Lauren and I were in bed with Moses, in our pajamas, ready for sleep. The trial was around the corner. Last-minute preparations for my defense were underway.

"Mike," my lawyer gushed, "our prayers have been answered! The government has decided to offer you a plea agreement in the zone of probation. They're giving you a level eleven, zone B plea. Exactly where we want to be!"

I was elated at the news. If I had pled guilty while still designated as a level twelve, Judge Wigenton would have had to sentence me to prison unless she went against the recommended sentencing guidelines. Now, those guidelines encouraged her to give me probation or community service rather than jail time. This meant I had a good chance of avoiding prison altogether, unless the judge decided to make an example out of me.

It was an amazing, monster moment for both me and Lauren. We had held out for so long, and this apparent victory was a culmination of our belief in each other and my hard work and dedication to doing the right thing.

I'd been volunteering at local high schools to speak about my story of experience, strength, and hope. I was also working at the treatment center where I had gotten clean once and for all, helping in small groups, counseling young men and women suffering from addiction. Assisting others fighting this vicious and debilitating disease had become my passion and was a big part of sober life. In recovery, it's called "service work." I wanted to give back. I believed putting all this positive energy into the universe was being reciprocated, and karma was starting to sway in my favor after almost three years of sobriety and being a constant force for good.

Lauren and I kissed and embraced, happy tears of joy wetting both our faces. Grinning, I told her we needed to celebrate with a photo of me (in my underwear) signing the plea bargain, where I pled guilty to a single count of tax evasion stemming from one year of my personal tax returns and that cash deposit.

We may just survive this thing after all, I thought as I signed the deal. It felt as if a giant weight had been lifted off my shoulders. This was another huge step toward putting the whole nightmare behind me. I couldn't help but be proud of myself and my actions in getting to this point.

Unfortunately, changing my plea from not guilty to guilty had unintended consequences. Now I belonged to the state. As I waited for sentencing, which would be about nine months later, the government placed travel restrictions on me. Any travel outside of the state of New Jersey would have to be approved by the judge. Judge Wigenton was notoriously strict, and if she denied my travel request, my comeback would be stopped before it even started. Filming for the new show would commence in days. If I couldn't travel, the new *Jersey Shore* project, along with any chance at redemption, would be in jeopardy.

But no matter. Life is 10 percent what happens to you and 90 percent how you react to it. This, too, I knew I would overcome. My plane ticket for Miami was booked. I even packed everything up before the court appearance where we would ask permission to travel. It was my way of projecting success and staying confident. The judge *had* to let me go.

Let's hope she agreed.

CHAPTER 26

A REBOOT AND A PROPOSAL

Any concerns about being denied permission to travel to Miami to film the new show quickly fell away at the designated court appearance. After seeing the progress I'd made in my life throughout the years this case had dragged on, the government had no objections to allowing me to travel for work. It made sense for them to let me go—they didn't want to limit my ability to earn a living, especially since my plea bargain included a $123,000 restitution payment. I made sure to take care of that immediately as a gesture to the court that I was accepting responsibility and taking my obligations seriously. Doing the next right thing.

Throughout all of this, I remained the model of sobriety. If I'd still been failing drug tests and acting a fool, there was no way my travel request would have been approved. In truth, they probably would have thrown me in jail already. But I was a proponent of "if you do good, you get good." And the good kept coming.

Because of the court appearance, I was a day or two behind my cast-mates arriving in Miami. Once doing so, it immediately felt like old times. Vinny and Pauly scooped me up at the airport, reuniting MVP. The three of us picked up right where we left off—breaking balls and laughing the entire car ride in. We were back to being our hilarious selves and making great TV the second that red light came on.

The three of us headed straight to The Clevelander, where our roommates were already who knows how many bottles of tequila deep. Right off the bat, I was facing my first hurdle. I won't lie, I was slightly concerned about being in that environment and potentially falling into old habits. You can see the worry on my face in that first episode. *What did I get myself into?*

Everyone was intoxicated with half naked girls all over. I realized I had to make an adjustment on the fly and acclimate myself to this challenging environment. To stay in my lane and run my own race. Instead of drinking—or worse—I instead chose to be in the moment, listen to the music, enjoy my friends' company, and order some chicken tendies and fries. The mindset was already there; I just needed to tap into it. By doing so, I was able to have a great time without being tempted by the crutch of intoxicants.

I got into bed that night in Miami feeling encouraged. The first obstacle had been overcome, and the warm reception from my roommates was incredibly encouraging and gracious. It proved that bygones were bygones. We were still family.

Our relationships would continue to blossom further as we went through that first season of *Jersey Shore: Family Vacation*, our chemistry picking right up where it had left off. In fact, those relationships grew stronger than they'd previously been, and eventually, Jenni referred me to her management company. In the never-ending quest for self-improvement, I sought small changes in my life wherever they presented themselves, and I thought this switch would be a positive one. I needed to put my career first and work with people who believed I could make this comeback happen. Robyn Bordes and Deven Turner with Illumination PR checked all those boxes.

Stepping into that South Beach party house, I did so as a completely different person from the one who'd entered the Seaside house so many years before. Like everyone else on the show, I had evolved. Those changes have been well-documented throughout the preceding pages and there is no need to belabor them further, but I both recognized and appreciated what a big moment this was for me. Not many had believed I would get back to this point. Even I'd harbored doubts.

When shooting began, I couldn't help but be overcome with excitement and pride over making it this far. My obsessive personality had nearly killed me; now, I was utilizing it to crush sobriety and life. I continued making the right decisions. Otherwise, this opportunity would never have come to fruition. And I felt very lucky it had. But they say luck is what happens when preparation meets opportunity, and I had been preparing for this moment for over two years. Each and every day, waking up and maintaining my positivity and optimistic outlook. Working hard. Doing the right things. Redirecting my obsessive personality, fine-tuning it, and turning it into my superpower. I—Big Daddy Sitch—was ready for this next chance. My first act had been legendary, but it was time to up my game. I knew it wouldn't be easy, but I also was confident I was up to the task.

At the same time, I was under no illusions that I was in the clear with my sobriety. The hard work was just beginning. I knew that what I was attempting would be my biggest challenge to date, and let's be honest, it was a recipe for disaster for maintaining sobriety. The first thing they teach you in recovery is to avoid temptations. Living in a party house and going to bars and clubs every night is a big no-no obviously. These activities are frowned upon in the recovery community, and I don't recommend that anyone struggling with addiction model this behavior.

But I had a different outlook. I had adopted a sober lifestyle and my own rigid set of principles, working my butt off to get where I was and to have this beautiful life. If I thought doing the show would jeopardize that, I wouldn't have participated. My sobriety and family remained my priorities. But I was willing to take the risk and bet on myself like I always had.

At the end of the day, my life is not cookie-cutter. When they created these sobriety commandments, they weren't thinking about the life of a reality TV star. I had to do what I had to do to provide for my family. But I knew I couldn't compromise on my own commandments. I had to stick with what had gotten me here.

The naysayers said there was no way I could stay sober in that environment. They said even if I could, a sober Mike wouldn't be entertaining and contribute to a hit show. I used it all as motivation. I actually relished the cameras being back on me 24/7. Video don't lie. The cameras would show whether I failed or prevailed. Any slipups, and the world would see it. I couldn't let that happen. I had to break the mold if I was going to prove everyone wrong.

Enter my next persona, The Designation. A complement to Big Daddy Sitch. When my roommates were drinking and partying, The Designation was the one taking care of them and driving everyone home safely. When they were in the club dancing with bottles of vodka, I was in the club dancing with Red Bull. Unencumbered by drugs or alcohol, I was able to take care of my friends. I was doing what they said couldn't be done: going out and having fun, smiling, dancing, being myself with no substances clouding my mind. I knew where drugs and alcohol took me. I wasn't going back there.

I not only proved it to my roommates and everyone watching on television, but I also proved it to myself. It was great. I was like, *wow*. I was having an amazing time, just on a vibe. I wasn't high—I was high on life. Listening to the music, drinking Diet Cokes. Fist pumping with an ear-to-ear grin. It actually seemed like I was having more fun than anyone else in the club. The naysayers were fucking with the wrong man. They didn't know the type of heart I had. I wasn't going to give up on myself.

That's not to say jumping back into *Jersey Shore* was all cake and roses. While things were great between me and Vinny, Pauly, Nicole, Jenni, and Deena, Ronnie and I did get into some heated arguments that first *Family Vacation* season. Coming from someone who knew the signs of addiction all too well, I could see that he needed help, and I told him he should go to rehab. He didn't appreciate my input, and fireworks ensued. Nothing new for me and Ronnie. But hey, things happen, and friction makes for good television. If anything, initially there was some concern that there wasn't enough.

Despite everyone being different people than we'd been during the first go-around, the squad was as it ever was. As much as everything had changed, nothing had changed. Our dynamic was the same. While I wasn't in perfect shape, I was in good enough shape. And though I didn't really identify as The Situation anymore and lived the mantra of keeping everything positive, I still wasn't afraid to speak my mind. I was confident this new version of Sitch still had the charisma and that "it" factor. However, to my surprise, one of the producers expressed some concern after my first interview of the season.

In these interviews, they make you articulate your emotions about what happened that day. *How did you feel about that interaction with JWoww or Pauly? What were you thinking when you first walked into the house?* And I remember during that first interview being slightly uncomfortable in front of the green screen. That sentiment surprised me because in my past life that had been where I did my best work.

Sev, a producer I'd known for at least a decade, pulled me aside. He was like, "Yo, Mike, is there something wrong? You're not yourself. You're one of the best to ever do this, and I'm just not feeling it."

Sev was right. I wasn't sure who I was trying to be. I thought doing the show would be like riding a bicycle. I'd been so good at being free and articulating how I felt during the first iteration of *Jersey Shore* that the camera and viewer could effortlessly relate to me. Everyone loved my interviews. They were hilarious and raw. Now that I was sober, it was different. That spark was still inside of me, I just had to remember how to pull it out without relying on chemicals to do so.

Simply put, what I needed was to be comfortable as this new persona I was developing into: Big Daddy Sitch, The Designation, The Inspiration. The former bad boy trying to be a good man. Someone who was in a committed relationship with his college sweetheart. That's who I was now.

After they pulled me aside and had that talk, it made me feel some type of way. I realized I needed to dig deep. I needed to find that strength inside of me to be comfortable with who I was at this particular time in my life. I needed to be vulnerable and embrace those vulnerabilities. To let the camera feel my exposedness and show the audience this very emotional period where I was rebuilding while at the same time living with this huge federal indictment hanging over my head. Fighting the mistakes of my past. *Jersey Shore* is a lifestyle show, a docufollow. People watching want to feel like they are part of our lives. I had to let them in.

I knew I could still be that funny guy. I could make light of things and be entertaining. And that's what I did—I turned those negative situations into positive situations and used them as fuel. In the end, once again, I broke the mold. I was making it happen. When the ratings came out, they confirmed the reboot was a hit. I was still a hit.

In the midst of this renaissance, I decided I was finally going to do something I'd always wanted to do. Lauren had seen me at my worst and pulled me through my darkest days. Now, she deserved me at my best. So I used the money I had earned from the show to buy her the ring of her dreams. Probably not the best business decision at the time, but fortunately assisted by a significant discount from the jeweler because of who I was.

I went to the producers and my roommates and told them that I wanted to propose to Lauren on the show. And that I wanted them to be a major part of it. Everyone was all for it—excited and supportive. It was up to me—with my best friends' assistance—to make this the proposal of the century. Lauren deserved that.

And that's what happened. It was a magical, special moment for us both. An amazing proposal in front of the people we loved, filmed for the world to see. Our engagement was the zenith of so many years of ups and downs. Good times and bad. We'd been through so much together. This grand ending wasn't guaranteed. In fact, the odds were stacked against us. But we'd made it. Lauren had loved me when I couldn't love myself. As I told her from one knee, she was my best friend, my college sweetheart, my better half, someone who made me a better person. She said yes!

Proposing on the reboot of the hit show that had made me a household name was incredibly sentimental. Making this memory on TV meant we could always watch it back and one day show our kids. I was so proud of how far we'd come. The happiness I felt being engaged to the love of my life, who had saved my life, made all the bad things I'd gone through to get here worth it. Lauren had shown me what living your best life truly was, and it wasn't the parties and the orgies and the drug-fueled nights. It was family and love. It was a strong relationship with God. I was so excited to start a family and spend the rest of our lives together.

But while we celebrated this happy time, those dark clouds that had been building for years finally settled overhead. The storm that was my legal woes arrived with a vengeance.

As Thanos said: "Dread it? Run from it? Destiny arrives all the same; now it's here."

CHAPTER 27
THE SENTENCE

The first season of the *Jersey Shore* reboot was a smash hit. *Family Vacation* was MTV's highest-rated new show in years. Two and half million people watched the premiere. Soon, contracts—and raises—for season two were put in front of us. Back to the races.

It was satisfying to know that my storylines were a big part of the show's draw and appeal. The proposal to Lauren had been great television, as was my pending court case. The whole country was watching, fascinated to find out whether The Situation was going to prison. I was there right there along with them.

Honestly, I was on cloud nine. Life was good. I had the woman I loved on my arm, I was back on the hit show that had started my career, making great money, and I was killing sobriety. With my guilty plea at a level that usually meant no jail time, the years-long legal case was finally behind us, or so we thought. I believed I had somehow made it through the inferno singed but unburnt. A rising phoenix.

As we began to shoot season two, the producers asked me what I wanted to do. I was like, "Let's put the pedal to the metal. Lauren and I are ready to get married. Let's start planning a wedding."

Lauren and I wanted to say "I do" as soon as possible. Believing the deal I had struck with the government meant probation, we were ready to reach the next phase and sail off into the sunset. As they were for most big moments of my adult life, the cameras, the country, and my castmates went along for the ride. I knew the world was watching as we visited wedding venues and tasted catering, and not only was I fine with it, I relished it. I wanted the audience to see me as this shining example of good. I felt like I had been assigned the mountain of addiction, bad decisions, and self-doubt to show others that it could be moved.

Lauren and I were so grateful and appreciative for this second chance. We had another shot at love, stardom, sobriety, and really, life in general.

This outcome had never been guaranteed. Far from it. But since it was here, Lauren and I couldn't wait to put down roots and start a family.

We put the final touches on the plans for our big day as my sentencing date approached. As we know, I was in the zone for probation and community service, and with no priors and all the changes I had made in my life, that was the outcome we all expected. However, there was always a chance Judge Wigenton, again, known for being very tough, could sentence me to prison. If she did, my understanding was that it would be the first time in New Jersey history a first-time offender in this zone would do jail time.

The night before sentencing, I remember standing in the shower, letting the hot water run over my head as steam filled the bathroom. MTV would be at the apartment early the next morning to film my journey to the courthouse. Lauren was in the bedroom, watching *The Crown* on Netflix as I concentrated on centering myself, preparing my mind for whatever would come the next day.

The next morning, when MTV showed up at the apartment to film me getting ready, SallyAnn Salsano, the executive producer of the show, someone who had been a fixture in my life since the inception of *Jersey Shore*, was in attendance. That alone told me what a big moment this was. I remember the worry and concern on her face but also the love and care she showed for me. I knew that whatever happened, I was not going to be disappointed. I was going to handle it with dignity. There was nothing more I could do.

As I buttoned my white Armani shirt and shouldered a dark gray suit, I felt goosebumps dot my arms. A warm chill ran down my spine. Still, I felt calm. I was at peace. There was a sense of serenity knowing I had done everything in my power to put myself in the best position to survive this. My fate was already sealed, even if I didn't know in which direction. This wasn't about winning. How can you win when you're being sentenced? It was about moving on with my life. This moment had been years in the making. I wasn't nervous for it; I was excited to confront my fate.

I think most people would be nervous and stressed walking into the same federal court building as so many infamous defendants had. MTV's camera crew remained in lockstep as paparazzi and fans swarmed the scene, shouting my name and asking questions. I remained unaffected. Cameras filming every aspect of my life was normal. People shouting at me on the street was normal. Flashbulbs in my face were normal. The whole thing may have been a circus, but nothing I wasn't used to. I could handle the pressure.

As Lauren and I approached the courthouse hand in hand, my cast-mates stood on the street in support, waiting for my arrival. I embraced each of my dear friends in a somber hug and made my way inside. It was time to learn my fate.

I was slightly concerned that the judge wouldn't appreciate all the cameras outside, but I didn't have any control over that. That was my job. It paid for my lawyers and was how I'd afforded the restitution I'd already made. I put it out of my mind and took my place at the defendant's bench.

I made eye contact with Vinny and Jenni, whom I'd chosen to come inside with me. My mom, sister, and brother Frank were there. Marc, my brother and co-defendant, sat on a separate bench in front of me.

Everyone looked pensive, especially Marc. Again, I was cool as a cucumber. What will be will be. I'd already battled and defeated my demons. Completing this next step meant I could move on with my life. I was ready to get it over with.

Judge Wigenton sentenced Marc first. She gave him twenty-four months in a federal prison like she was handing out candy.

Damn, Marc must have taken the hit, was my immediate thought. He was more involved in the business and a level thirteen, which was not even close to probation on the sentencing table, but still, that sentence was more than we expected. I figured if they gave him two years, they weren't going to send me to prison too.

It was my turn.

"Will the defendant please rise." The words seemed to echo across the crowded courtroom. I stood, calm and collected. My senses were heightened. It felt like I could hear every murmur in the crowd, feel any circulation of air. Even the light seemed brighter, more crisp. I noticed the court reporter typing, an artist in the corner drawing my picture. I took a deep breath.

Judge Wigenton looked down upon me and stated, "While I am quite moved by Mr. Sorrentino's sobriety and progress these last few years, he still needs to be accountable for actions years ago. That is why I am recommending to the court that he serve eight months in prison, no less than two years of probation, and five hundred hours of community service."

There were gasps in the audience. It felt like the air had been sucked from the room. I had an almost out-of-body experience, as if I were watching myself receive the sentence. My mom, sister, and brother Frank all started crying. So did Jenni. Lauren was visibly and understandably devastated. I saw Vinny with his head down in disbelief.

I didn't react. I remained calm. Steadfast and stoic. I refused to be upset. *Okay, I guess we're doing this now.* I even wondered to myself in those first few seconds, once again, *Why am I emotionless?* My brain was processing a sentence that it hadn't seen coming. It's not fully accurate to say I was blindsided because we always knew this was, though unlikely, a remote possibility. But in that moment, I knew I had a choice in how I handled it. I could either lie down and die or take my medicine and be a man and rise above it.

I chose the latter. I knew it wasn't going to be easy to walk this road, but then it dawned on me why I was taking it in such stride. All the pain and suffering I'd endured over the years had prepared me for this. Nothing was as hard as getting and staying sober. I welcomed this next challenge. I was going to use this fresh pain as fuel to continue my journey of self-improvement. Prison was simply going to be my next chapter.

I told myself, no matter what, I wasn't going to get distraught. I'd already been through all the hard work. I'd had the sleepless nights. The months of not believing in myself and thinking I was a failure. Sitting there, even after learning I would be going to prison for eight months, I refused to hang my head. On the contrary, it remained elevated. I thought myself a champion for coming out the other side. I felt like God had brought me through the storm, and these little raindrops weren't going to faze me.

Like a great man once said (many, many times): the comeback is always greater than the setback.

Vinny Guadagnino, Jersey Shore *castmate:*

MTV wanted the show to have representation at Mike's sentencing, but obviously, cameras weren't allowed in the courtroom. I don't know if it was Mike or MTV who selected me and Jenni as the cast members to attend, but at least they knew enough not to send all eight of us in there. We tend to be a bit of a traveling circus wherever we go, and that probably wouldn't have been the best look for the judge. When you have a celebrity sitting there, you know they want to make an example out of him. Bringing in a bunch of reality stars probably wouldn't help. I have a political science degree and kind of look like a nice, young gentleman, so I guess that's why they picked me to go in while the rest of the cast watched outside.

We weren't sure what to expect. I knew Mike was in the zone for probation, and after listening to his lawyer break down the case during his opening argument, I was convinced that's all he should get. His lawyer was good, explaining to the courtroom that if Mike was sent to prison for this, it would be the first time in the state of New Jersey that someone in these circumstances did time. By the end of his speech, my hopes were certainly up.

Of course, the prosecutor was nearly as convincing, recommending a lengthy jail sentence. When the lawyers finished doing their thing, the judge told Mike to rise. He had a fresh suit on, a clean haircut. Mike looked like he was using that courtroom for a photo shoot. I remember how relaxed and indifferent he seemed. Jenni and I definitely appeared more nervous than Mike. I couldn't believe how nonchalant he was with his life hanging in the balance.

Then, the judge read the sentence. Eight months in prison. My jaw dropped. It was kind of like, BAM! Like watching a basketball game where your team just lost the championship by one point on a last-second half-court shot. It was heartbreaking. We were almost there. We thought we'd won. But no, it was a last-minute, soul-crushing loss. My first thought was, *Damn, Mike has to go to jail.* That realization was immediately followed by, *How's he going to handle it?*

I should have known the answer. He handled it like he'd handled everything over the past few years—like a G. I was watching him intently as the judge announced the sentence, and he didn't even flinch when she dropped the hammer. It was like he had already accepted whatever the outcome was going to be. This guy had just been told he was going to prison, and he didn't even react. He held his head high and just accepted it. But that's Mike. It's in his character. He does it with everything. He doesn't try to control the situation; he just accepts it.

I make fun of him for having a short attention span, like Dory from *Finding Nemo*, just floating around out there. But it's a huge strength. Mike is always in the moment, a very present guy. Whatever hell he went through during his recovery, he applies those lessons to every aspect of his life. He took his sentencing like he took everything: one day at a time.

We filmed the next day, and I remember being scared about what it was going to be like interacting with a guy who had just been sentenced to prison. But he was just Mike. The same guy as always. Making the same jokes, laughing about Secaucus, treating it like any other day. I had to respect his attitude.

A couple months later, on the day he reported to prison, Lauren texted the group with an update: "He's inside. First thing he did was get a haircut. Now he changed into his comfies and is drinking diet soda." I laughed, like, this kid is going to be fine.

CHAPTER 28

"TAKE ME TO JAIL"

While my fiancée, friends, and family wept outside the courtroom, a bailiff escorted me downstairs to the bowels of the courthouse for processing. The cops seemed apologetic as they took my mugshot and fingerprints, treating me with the utmost respect through each step. One of them smiled at me ruefully and said, "Sorry that we gotta do this, Mike." I nodded, explaining I understood he was just doing his job and that I appreciated the professionalism. Even amidst the drama and disappointment of what had just transpired, it still felt good to be liked.

As they led me through intake, Marc turned a corner, and we came face to face with each other. Our eyes met, and we shared a knowing smirk. The silent communication that passed between us did so as it only can with brothers. It was as if we were saying to each other, "At least we're not going through this alone. We have each other." It reminded me of when we were kids and did everything together except, you know, this time, it was prison instead of a taekwondo tournament. But there was an odd comfort knowing we'd be sharing this prison experience with one another, though ultimately at different facilities.

Despite the courtroom results, I wasn't dejected. I was taking accountability. I knew none of this would have happened if I'd been sober and my best self so many years before. This entire debacle had occurred due to my carelessness and recklessness. By not being on top of my employees and neglecting the details of my business, I was the one responsible. My name was the one at the top of all the accounts, and ultimately, it had been my duty to see they were properly managed. I was going to take my medicine like a man, standing tall and remaining positive while doing so. Continuing down this path of self-improvement was very empowering.

Before we left the courtroom that day, I made sure to stop at the cashier's booth and pay the $10,000 fine the judge had issued at sentencing. Then, Lauren and I left the courthouse just as we had entered it several hours before: hand in hand, heads held high. The judge had given me time at home to get my affairs in order before I had to report to prison, and I intended to use that time to its full potential. Most importantly, to wed my beautiful fiancée. The clock was ticking.

Our ride home (with MTV filming inside the car) was sobering, pun intended. For an addict, getting unexpected bad news like a prison sentence can easily lead to a relapse. I'm proud to say never once did I think to get high or take a drink.

That's not to say I was totally unaffected by what had transpired in that courtroom. On the contrary, once I finally plopped on the couch next to Lauren and Moses that night, mental and physical exhaustion set in. I felt like I'd been knocked down in a prizefight. The ref was standing over me with an eight count while I searched for my mouthpiece, dizzy and battered. But I wasn't KO'd. I knew I had to get up, both literally and metaphorically. At that moment, I went to one knee. I clenched my eyes tight and said a prayer to God before rising to my feet.

How would I cope with this defeat? The old Sitch might have relapsed and possibly never come back from it. What would the new Sitch do? I'll tell ya: Big Daddy Sitch, The Designation, The Inspiration, filled a huge bowl with salty, unhealthy snacks, poured a large Diet Coke, and curled back up on the couch with his loved ones. For the next twenty-four hours, Lauren and I watched movies and relaxed while contemplating what had just occurred and where we would go from here. We worked hard to avoid all the coverage of my trial, which was on every channel. Many questions with few answers swirled around. Was the wedding off? Delayed? What about my job? Would MTV wait for me? Would the show get canceled?

As we contemplated those scenarios, I didn't try to escape from my feelings of loss; in fact, I did the opposite. I stayed in the defeat, relishing the painful emotions coursing through my body. I wanted to taste them, to smell them. To remember what this felt like. Because I *never* wanted to feel it again. This defeat would be transferred into motivation. I allowed myself to stay down for those first twenty-four hours. But when they were over, I got up, knowing I was now somehow fundamentally different. It was as if my broken pieces had been transformed into a masterpiece.

The next day, there was a knock at our door. When I opened it, a full ensemble of my castmates stood on the threshold. I'd forgotten that we had scheduled a party for the day after trial, based on the presumption I would get probation and/or community service. I'd assumed the celebration would be off since the worst scenario possible had transpired. But nope, there they were, on my doorstep, cast and crew ready to film. This was important content for the show, and I had a job to do.

As much as I wanted space in the moment, their arrival turned out to be a good thing. The love and support of my best friends meant a lot to me. The squad brought all my favorite snacks over, and we sat around laughing while Ronnie told us a tale about getting jumped in Secaucus the night before. Secaucus? Lol. The crew decided to head out to Stewart's Root Beer, and I told Lauren to stay in bed and relax with Moses while I went downstairs to have lunch with everyone.

When I walked through the door, everyone shouted, "You popped your cherry!" just like the scene in *Goodfellas* after Henry Hill got arrested for the first time. I couldn't help but laugh. I loved it. To be honest with you, at that moment, the pressure and disappointment of the past twenty-four hours sort of melted away. It was therapeutic to be busy again and working. Filming with my friends took my mind off everything. Again, my storyline was a big part of the show, and it was important to me that we continued telling my tale. I wanted the public to see how well I was handling this latest adversity. It didn't hurt that a Nielsen poll was released about this same time listing me as one of the top reality stars on social media.

That week, I reached an infallible decision. I refused to allow these circumstances to define me. Instead, I defaulted to my standard operating procedure of being grateful. Simply trying to improve myself and being my best every single day. A prison sentence wasn't going to change the mentality that got me here. If anything, it was going to make me more committed to becoming the best version of myself that I could. These were the cards I'd been dealt; I was determined to play the shit out of them.

Lauren and I informed MTV that with a looming jail term, we intended to get married as soon as possible. Naturally, the ceremony would be a part of the show, and production would be involved. I was committed to giving my sweetheart the wedding of her dreams—she certainly deserved it. I may have been the one going to prison, but make no mistake about it, Lauren would have to do hard time as well.

Our top choice for a wedding destination was Italy, but due to my travel restrictions, that wasn't possible. Instead, we found the next best thing: the most amazing venue in Pompton Plains, New Jersey, called The Legacy Castle. I felt so fortunate to be able to leverage my celebrity status and employer to make this the most over-the-top dream wedding we could imagine.

If you haven't seen "The Hitch-uation" episodes on *Family Vacation,* you can't imagine how ridiculous this place and the entire wedding was. (The first time I saw them was in the prison cafeteria on one of the televisions the Russians controlled; luckily, the Russians liked me and put the show on.) The venue was beyond gorgeous. Everything about our wedding was over the top. Incredible food and desserts, as you'd expect. Performers hanging from the ceilings. A live band. Pauly and MTV even organized a surprise celebrity performance of Rob Base singing "It Takes Two" while RSVP and I executed a choreographed dance. Lauren was completely surprised and blown away. We had the most amazing time while focusing on being in the moment and not worrying about what was to come.

Having my castmates be such a big part of our day was incredibly meaningful, as was MTV filming everything, allowing the fans to share in our happiness. Jenni's and Nicole's daughters walked down the aisle as flower girls, while Ronnie, Pauly, and Vinny, along with Marc, were my best men. It was a testament to how far these relationships had come and would continue to strengthen.

After the wedding, Lauren I honeymooned at an amazing resort in Arizona called Miraval, where we were pampered for a week—facials, massages, private chefs, the whole experience. The resort even surprised us with a Funfetti cake upon arrival. It was another amazing opportunity available because of the show, and we were extremely appreciative of all of it.

When we returned home, I continued prioritizing what was important. The judge had extended my prison report date to January to allow me to get married and spend the holidays with my family, which I was also incredibly grateful for. I spent the time with my new bride living in the moment—and making sure I ate well. I knew that soon the foods I enjoyed would no longer be available, so I vowed to never skip dessert and eat that extra slice while I still could. There were no leftovers on my plate as I prepared to do time, though maybe a few extra jiggles around the waistline.

As my report date got closer and closer and closer, I never once felt sorry for myself. At the time, we were still in negotiations with MTV for the next season of *Jersey Shore: Family Vacation* as well as for Lauren to get her own contract. I could rest easy knowing that once those deals were in place, my wife would be well taken care of with me in prison.

Finally, the day arrived. I was to report to jail and start my time. Eight months in a federal prison camp. A punishment years in the making, this would be the final step before I could move on with my life. I was ready to pay my debt to society.

I woke up early that morning, about six o'clock. I hadn't slept well, tossing and turning for most of my final night on a comfortable mattress for the foreseeable future. I got up, brushed my teeth, dressed in a comfy sweatsuit, and tweeted the GIF of Ray Liotta in *Goodfellas*: "Now take me to jail."

The car that would do so arrived at our apartment around seven in the morning. Lauren and I went downstairs and were greeted by TMZ, whom we tried to duck, and Deven, my publicist, who joined us in the car. Since we were still in negotiations with MTV, their producers and cameras didn't ride with us, instead following behind and filming from a distance.

The drive to Federal Correctional Institution Otisville in rural New York was a long one. Both Lauren and Deven filmed the journey on their iPhones, and I even went live on the 'Gram to say goodbye to my fans and assure them that The Situation—now under construction—was going to be back bigger and better than ever.

During the three-and-a-half-hour drive, my thoughts mostly revolved around, *How am I going to say goodbye to the love of my life?* I wasn't worried about actually being in prison. I had a sense of security that I could handle whatever would come my way. There was a peace knowing I could no longer do anything about it. I was going to prison, and that was that. My main concern centered around Lauren and whether she was going to be okay with me gone. It would be just her and Moses. I worried about them both. But like me, there was nothing she could do except remain strong. I had no doubt about the strength we both possessed.

As we approached the turnoff for the prison, a heavy police presence grew more visible, only growing stronger the closer we got to the facility. Press and paparazzi lined the country roads until, finally, we reached a roadblock set up specifically for my arrival. It was crazy out there with everyone waiting for me. Our car pulled up to the checkpoint, I rolled down my window, and they waved us through once they saw it was me. No ID needed.

The driver parked at the prison gates. I knew this was going to be the hardest part. It was time to say goodbye to my wife, a heartbreaking prospect for us both. I forced myself to remain positive on the outside, but on the inside, at that moment, I was breaking down. I was ashamed to be putting my new wife through this. When Lauren started to tear up, I reached over to give her a quick hug and kiss but had to immediately break contact. I didn't want to go inside looking a mess, so I was very mindful to not get too emotional during our goodbye. Walking into any prison with tears in your eyes is never a good idea, even if it's a low-security camp like Otisville.

Nonetheless, my eyes shimmered slightly as I whispered to my bride one of the many inspirational quotes I often utilized to help us through each trial (literally) and tribulation: "We didn't come this far just to come this far." I wholly believed in each saying and relied on them like protective armor. I then let go of her hand, turned around, and walked through the prison gates, head held high. I didn't look back.

The door slammed shut behind me, locking with what seemed to be a deafening finality.

CHAPTER 29
WELCOME TO OTISVILLE

I quickly gathered my composure upon entering the walls of my new home. As I said, I wasn't about to walk into prison with tears in my eyes. Though I couldn't help feeling emotional about leaving my new wife, I knew I had to bury those sentiments. They wouldn't do me any good in here. So I pushed down the nearly overwhelming sense of guilt and anger at my former self for robbing me and my wife of this time together. We should have been enjoying life at home as newlyweds; instead, I was checking into prison while she was taking the long drive home. Alone.

I wasn't sure what I expected prison to be like. Otisville was a minimum-security camp, so it's not like I was walking into Shawshank. But I'd watched enough prison movies to know danger lurked around each corner. And what did Shawshank teach us? That the guards could be just as dangerous as the inmates.

As I signed in and handed over my wallet, identification, and clothes, those fears racing through my head were quickly assuaged. Just like when I was processed at the courthouse after sentencing, the prison guards couldn't have been more courteous and respectful. As I prepared for the mandatory strip search, naked, I couldn't help but be mindful of how uncomfortable a situation this could be. I knew there was a potential to be violated, but that's not at all what happened. Instead of being treated inhumanely, like an animal, it was the opposite. Truth be told, I was taken aback at how nice everyone was.

The day after Christmas, a couple weeks before I reported, Lauren had received a long DM from a woman claiming that her husband was an inmate in Otisville. We obviously get DMs all the time, but this one seemed legitimate. The woman said the inmates had been informed I would be joining them and that her husband, Andy, a fellow Italian, would take me under his wing. She gave Lauren the lay of the land:

what to expect on visitations, some tips on how to deposit money into my commissary account, and how often I would be able to communicate. She told us her husband had offered to have a list of items I would need waiting for me immediately upon arrival, "no strings attached lol."

Lauren and I were skeptical, and again, having completed the canon of HBO prison shows, I knew accepting gifts in prison was a bad idea. But the woman seemed nice, and her messages sounded sincere, so Lauren told her she appreciated the help and even gave her my shoe size. The woman told Lauren that Andy would have a pair of sneakers, as well as sweatpants, sweatshirt, and toiletries, waiting for me when I got there since commissary wasn't available during the first two weeks of incarceration.

Now, with prison intake completed, outfitted in my prison greens (the same outfit I would wear for the duration of my stay), I was about to enter the dormitory where all the prisoners lived. I was interested to see what type of greeting I would get. The woman's messages echoed in my head. Was this guy from an apparently "(semi lol) normal Italian family" who was in on conspiracy charges really trying to be my friend or just trying to take advantage of me? Uncle Nino said he'd put the word out for people he knew in there to take care of me, but I had no idea if that was true.

As I walked "up the hill"—the climb leading from the prison admin offices to the dorms, a wooded path that reminded me of the grounds of a large high school—my head was on a swivel. By the time I reached the top of the hill, the unknown had faded away. Andy Cucumbers was waiting for me with a duffel bag the size of a hockey goalie's. (The commissary the Italians had waiting for me was not exclusive to reality stars—each demographic usually put together care packages for their new arrivals. I would do so for several later arrivals. It's called "paying it forward.") All the things Lauren had put on the list for Andy's wife were in that bag: Reeboks, socks, sweats, new T-shirts, deodorant, shampoo, etc. It was a lifesaver lending to an immediate sense of camaraderie. Guys took care of their own in there. It wasn't what I was expecting at all.

Andy gregariously introduced himself, and we became fast friends. He was in his mid-forties, about the same height as me—five-foot-eleven—with a slight belly and bald head. I discovered Andy was a hustler and ran the kitchen in there. On the streets, he had led a multi-million-dollar interstate fencing ring, which is what landed him in Otisville.

I'd soon come to find out just how powerful his job in the kitchen made Andy. Food was currency in prison, and working in the kitchen meant you were the banker. Since Andy and his Italian compatriot in the kitchen, Tony Meatballs, liked me, I ate as good as you possibly could in there. They'd sneak me out protein so I could stick to my diet—chicken, tuna, mackerel, whatever they had. I even received custom, fresh salads.

I settled into prison quickly. First day, first thing? A haircut. That's right—they had a barber shop in there, and I got a #1 fade and shape-up twice a week. Prison or not, you know I had to stay fresh to death. It was one of the things I did to make the place my own, along with working out and eating as well as I could. A guy named Elvis also did my laundry in exchange for commissary. Small comforts like these made the time go as smoothly as possible.

Thankfully, everyone in there was familiar with my redemption story and liked me because of it. They watched the show and knew I had turned over a new leaf and recently gotten married. Everyone wanted to take care of me. They were rooting for me.

My counselor, a super nice Italian guy, was a big fan. When it came time to be assigned a job (everyone in Otisville had to have one), he told me I would be working under "Jimmy," who would "take care of" me. Wink wink. Jimmy didn't make me do shit, and everyone just left me alone to do my time as I saw fit.

I already mentioned how ingratiated I was with the kitchen crew. The people who ran that place loved me. Same with the dorms. I got a choice bunk—in the corner so I had a little bit of privacy. Well, as much privacy as is possible when sharing a large room with dozens of other men. They even gave me a new mattress instead of an old, thin one like most inmates had. It was no Sealy Posturepedic, but at least I was getting the best of the worst. Making the most out of a horrible situation.

Most new guys had to search for their seats in the cafeteria and could easily be told they weren't allowed to occupy certain tables. But the Russians who ran things looked out for me and invited me to sit with them. I even ended up learning a little Russian from guys with names like Crazy Alex. They gave me the lay of the land and told me who to stay away from. If there was ever an issue, which there rarely was, they handled it for me.

Once, after I'd been there a few months, a new Russian showed up. I think he'd come from a "real" prison and must have behaved well enough to be transferred to the camp. This dude was pretty old, but he was also shredded. I'm talking *Men's Health* jacked.

His first day there, this new comrade told me that from now on, I would have to give him my breakfast every morning. I was like, "Hold up. What did you say? You're taking my oatmeal and fruit? Nah, hell no!"

The next morning, he came up to me. "Where's my breakfast?" he asked.

I sneered at him. "Your breakfast? This is my breakfast. You ain't getting it."

He walked away. I wasn't sure if it was over or if we were going to have to settle this in the back of the gym, where most fights occurred. We called it "shooting the fair one." But I guess that by standing up to him, he knew I wasn't a mark, and he didn't try to get my breakfast again. Maybe it was a test to see how I would react. The Russians did have a little sit-down about it, but in the end, it was all good. Me and that guy actually became friends and would lift together.

But it really wasn't that type of prison. A few times people got smacked, and if the assaulter got caught, he might get locked down in the special housing unit (SHU) for a couple of days. If they found you with contraband like a phone or drugs, you could get sent to the SHU for up to a month or even transferred next door to the medium-security prison. That's what you really didn't want to have happen. That was a real prison with violent offenders. It may even have been where the attempted breakfast bandit had come from, I'm not sure. But our facility didn't even have fences or barbed wire. You didn't want to get sent away from the camp, which is why I was a model prisoner, walking the straight and narrow the entire time I was in there.

But that's what happened to Billy McFarland, the Fyre Festival guy. I remember the day he arrived at Otisville, the guys put cheese sandwiches on his bunk as a joke. You know, the same food he supposedly fed the people at the faux music festival he put on in the Bahamas, which is what landed him in prison for fraud. He laughed the joke off, not that he had much choice.

Billy was a loner in Otisville who pretty much kept to himself. We played basketball together a few times, but he wasn't very social. His girlfriend would come visit, and they were very nice to me and my wife, but that was the extent of our relationship.

He didn't last in Otisville long. Billy was caught with a USB drive, which was contraband, and sent to solitary in the SHU for like three months before getting transferred to another prison. Billy said the drive was to record notes for his book, but the whispers were that he was trying to secretly record other prisoners. Allegedly, of course.

After he got out, Billy actually DM'd me and asked if I wanted to work with him on his new venture. Lauren and I sort of chuckled at the offer. It was nice that he thought of me, but I didn't return the message. We didn't think being associated with the next Fyre Festival would be on brand for me.

The guy who had hacked Jennifer Lawrence's nudies was also in there. George was a nice kid who'd made some mistakes, like everyone else. We used to play Scrabble together. There were a couple billionaires in Otisville too I believe. Michael Cohen, President Trump's former lawyer who was sentenced to three years for tax evasion, was probably the biggest name to appear at Otisville during my time.

I remember a buzz permeated the facility in the days leading up to Michael Cohen's arrival. We could hear helicopters overhead, which I assume were the media trying to get a glimpse of this polarizing figure checking into prison.

I met Michael that first day, and we hit it off. He was a nice guy and told me that we'd met before. I wasn't sure if it was during *Dancing with the Stars* or at the Trump roast, but sometime during that era. My memory from those days was a little hazy, and I didn't remember the meeting, but it was nice he did. Little did he know, people tell me something similar almost daily.

The same groups who took me in—the Russians and Italians—also befriended Mike Cohen. While known as a facility for high-profile prisoners, Otisville was also a destination for Jewish prisoners because there was a kosher kitchen. Mike would often get a kosher meal, then take his tray to my table to eat lunch and dinner. We sat together for every meal, talking about life and politics and all the other things bored, notorious men talk about while being held against their will. He made it clear he was no longer a fan of Mr. Trump while also giving me advice on things like writing a book.

When he first got there, I heard that Mike didn't eat chicken, that he'd had one as a pet or something as kid. Being on my diet, I was always on the prowl for extra clean protein. Well, the best meal in that place, by far, was on Thursdays. We called it Chicken Thursday, and we'd get a quality piece of meat for dinner. Let me tell you, that chicken breast was a hot commodity in there. I called Mike Cohen over on his first Chicken Thursday. I put my hand on his shoulder, making some deep and serious eye contact. "Mike, I'm gonna need you to hook me up with your piece of chicken," I told him. "Just put it in my locker, and I'll grab it later."

"Oh yeah, Mike, no problem," he crowed. "Anything for you!"

Cool, I thought, excited for that extra protein. That evening, I kept an eye out for Mike at the main cafeteria, but there was no sign of him. *What the hell? Where is my chicken?*

I finally caught up to him. "Mike, what the fuck, man? Where is my chicken?"

"Ah, man, they're onto us!" he exclaimed, all nervous. "They knew I was gonna smuggle you that chicken. I woulda gotten caught!"

I always got a kick out of that story. But Michael Cohen and I got along well, and I heard he even mentioned me in his book, saying I was the most positive guy he'd ever been around. I take pride in that because spreading that positive attitude in prison was a gift I tried to bestow upon the other prisoners. Some guys would just stare at the walls and be miserable, but that wasn't me. You have a choice in prison: you can cry about your circumstances, or you can put forth the effort to improve yourself. I not only chose the latter, I tried to help others do the same.

Any time that I felt a wave of depression or weakness, I'd use the pain as fuel to give me strength. I can't tell you how many times in prison I flashbacked to watching my wife walk down the aisle to visualize how beautiful she was. Sometimes, during a workout, a tear would escape as I thought back to that special day, which was natural for someone using his emotions as motivation.

I received a ton of mail in prison, which helped keep my spirits high. The love and support from so many fans around the world was unreal. Strangers would send me magazines, letters, and other reading material. It helped make my time inside bearable, not only having new magazines, but being able to share them with the other inmates. Being a happily married man, any inappropriate bikini photos or the like would get eagerly claimed by the other guys.

One day early on, the warden came to see me. He told me that so much mail had come in for me that it shut down the mail room. I was flattered but also a little nervous. What would the other inmates think? Now they weren't getting their mail. I had no control over it, but still, I hoped I didn't get into a confrontation over it. But the guys were cool about the whole thing and kept it moving.

Most of my time in prison was dedicated to getting back into amazing shape. That was a promise I'd made to myself before I went in—that I would use the time to better myself in every way possible: mentally, spiritually, personally, professionally, and especially physically. Because by the time I arrived at prison, I was in terrible shape. Combine not going to the gym for months with a poor diet, and The Situation was fully under construction.

A huge black guy named Tyshaun ran the gym, which was old and dungeon-like. When I first got there, it was explained to me that you couldn't just work out whenever you wanted. Certain guys and groups had rights at certain times, and you couldn't just go whenever you felt like it. But I was like, "Yo, I gotta get in there. I gotta get back in shape." The gym—the weights, the bars, the iron—was where I felt most comfortable. I knew the proper etiquette and had no issues working out whenever I needed to.

When I first arrived, I couldn't even bench 135 pounds. By the time I left, I was doing 315. I went from 220 pounds to 185 in those eight months. A ton of hard work went into that transformation.

I would get up at seven in the morning and do an hour of fast cardio on the treadmill or walk around the yard. I'd come back and have my protein shake and breakfast, then take a little nap. After lunch, I'd lift for at least an hour or two in the gym, which had limited equipment but enough to get the job done. Andy Cucumbers worked out with me every day; since he helped me with extra food, I helped him get in shape. After lifting, there would be another protein shake. Then, I'd read the Bible or a fitness magazine before dinner at four o'clock. They always had TMZ on during dinner, and there were plenty of times I'd see myself on there, which I always got a kick out of. As I said, Andy and Tony Meatballs would usually sneak me some extra protein or a cucumber and tomato salad, and then, before final count, I'd do another round of cardio, usually wind sprints. Abs every other day.

As I said, this man was on a mission. A fire burned inside me, and the clock was ticking. I knew I only had a certain amount of time before the big reveal. The world was watching. By this point, we had our new contracts and significant raises from MTV, and my release from prison would be televised. I wanted everyone to see the great shape I was in, to see how I had utilized my time inside.

Other than that, I kept my head down and my spirits high. I remained on my best behavior. Mentally, staying sober was a task in itself. Guys definitely smuggled drugs in there, but I was never tempted. I'd come too far to turn back. The only thing I took was melatonin to sleep. My biggest infraction was securing some smuggled-in pre-workout supplements, which was a hot commodity in there.

I didn't allow my parents or siblings to visit me. Prison wasn't a fun place to be, and I didn't want their presence to make me feel soft or emotional in any way. I spoke on the phone with my mom as well as all my castmates, who were filming and getting ready for my return to the show. There was a computer room open during certain times that I could use to communicate with my loved ones via the Department of Corrections' email system.

What I looked forward to the most (aside from my release date) were Lauren's visits. She made the three-and-a-half-hour drive for visitation at least once or twice a week the entire time I was locked up. She'd usually have tears in her eyes when she arrived, and I could tell that her spirits were low. It was my job to bring her up. I was like a motivational speaker during those visits. It was imperative that I remain a beacon of positivity, so I made sure to stay extremely upbeat and uplifting. I was very empathetic to what she was going through, alone at home with only Moses while taking care of the home front. Our family was on hold while I did my penance. We both had to walk our own journeys by ourselves, and I felt guilt and shame at having put her in this position. It could easily have been demoralizing if we let it.

But we didn't. We continued to move forward with grace and class as the world watched. I was super proud of both myself and my wife. We were going to survive, and I was going to do my time and remain sober. We stayed loving and supportive through these tough tests.

And finally, after eight months as a guest of the government in Federal Correctional Institution Otisville, I had my release date: September 12, 2019. It was gratifying to know I'd done my full time like a man—taking it bell to bell, as they say. Sleeping in a dorm with fifty other guys who maybe weren't all focused on their hygiene. The bad food, the thin mattress, the same ill-fitting green uniform every single day. Showering with a towel that was perpetually wet (I can still smell it to this day). Constant counts to make sure no one had escaped. All that was finally over, and I could move forward with my life and wife.

That final night in prison, I lay awake all night, almost finding it hard to believe this horrific ordeal was hours away from being behind me. Knowing that I'd handled it admirably was extra rewarding. It was like Christmas morning times infinity.

Happiness flooded me. The next morning, I'd have my freedom back.

CHAPTER 30
A NEW CHAPTER

The excitement pulsing through me that final night in Otisville dissipated little with the sun's leisurely arrival. I popped out of my metal bunk, slightly in disbelief that this nightmare was about to be over. I'd not merely endured another traumatic ordeal but thrived over the past eight months. I was still sober, again shredded, and always cheerful. My attitude remained buoyed by gratitude and positivity. It was as if I'd built a house with the bricks thrown at me.

This is probably a good time to give my parents their due credit. I don't know that I would have survived addiction and prison without the morals and values they instilled in me, not to mention the tough love administered throughout my life. I believe my upbringing was what provided the strength and toughness required to get through it all.

I had asked Lauren to bring a T-shirt emblazoned with my now famous quote, "The Comeback Is Always Greater Than the Setback," when she came to pick me up. It was important to me to be wearing that shirt when I exited prison. I knew how much I would be photographed and filmed that day, and I wanted to spread the positivity outside the prison walls, just as I had inside them. Lauren and I had also started a T-shirt company, so hey, a little free advertising didn't hurt.

When I first caught a glimpse of my bride as a free man, I thought my heart would burst from happiness and my cheeks explode from smiling. I was over the moon. I wrapped Lauren in an enormous hug, wiped her tears, and kissed her deeply. Like we'd done so many times before, each one of us took the other's hand. Fingers interlocked and melded into a single devoted entity, we walked past the razor wire lining the main prison facility, officially putting this bad situation behind us. I leaned over to my wife and whispered, "We did it, honey." I then raised my finger to the sky in a tribute to the Almighty as a demonstration of my appreciation, knowing the world was watching.

219

MTV was filming the entire procession, and a producer immediately popped out of the woodwork to mic me up. We were led to a waiting SUV, also rigged for video and audio, and just like that, I was back in the swing of things. Five minutes outside of prison and I was back at work.

The Situation's release was world news. Press and paparazzi were camped outside the prison perimeter, but I was so happy, I barely noticed. MTV had a veritable army awaiting my exit, and I couldn't help but think how strange all this was. I recognized that most people didn't have this type of circus waiting for them when they left prison, and it felt a little surreal, like so many parts of my existence. Most of my adult life had been documented for public consumption, so being on camera thirty seconds after getting released from prison didn't feel like a big deal to me. It was back to the grind. There were benefits to having a huge company like MTV pick you up though; they had several cars and production vans in wait, and our drivers were able to throw off the paparazzi with some evasive driving on the way home. I thought that was pretty cool.

Once we settled onto the highway, I immediately jumped on group chat and texted my roommates, who were already in the midst of filming the next season of *Jersey Shore: Family Vacation*. "I'm free, bitch!" I exclaimed, and the back and forth began. I would meet up with them in the coming days at a house in Manalapan where filming had begun. The relationships with my castmates had grown even closer during my time away. Each one of them had made the trip to visit me in Otisville, and it was heartwarming and flattering that they showed that support.

After texting the crew from the car, I next called my mom, and then, as we got closer to Jersey, Denino's Pizza in Aberdeen. I pretty much ordered everything on their menu: a large vodka pizza, a large plain, a large margherita, and a sausage and peppers pizza. I also got a chicken parm sub, chicken fingers and fries, mozzarella sticks, and two or three diet sodas. All I wanted to do was get home, see Moses, eat good food, and make sweet love to my wife while cherishing every second.

MTV was very accommodating, but at the end of the day, they didn't want to miss anything. Though they were empathetic and sensitive of the moment, I did get a little pushback once we got home and I wanted to take some time for my newfound freedom to sink in. I appreciated where they were coming from; we both had a job to do, and theirs was to document everything that was going on with my release. I understood that and had no problem with it. In fact, I wanted my story on camera to ensure it was told accurately. The reboot was garnering huge numbers, and we needed to keep the momentum, especially with my prison storyline in full swing. The comeback would be televised, and I was in complete cooperation.

Lauren and I knew we wanted to start a family right away and had discussed laying down roots and moving out of the apartment we enjoyed so much. She had been looking at houses in Holmdel while I was gone and told me joyfully she'd found our dream home. When I saw it a few weeks later, I was sold. After years of planning and making good decisions, we finally moved into the house of our dreams.

It was a very exciting time. Though I was still on probation and had five hundred hours of community service to complete, prison was behind us. I was coming up on four years sober and had started Recovery Inc., a company where I consulted at rehab facilities around the country. I worked with small groups, doing promotions and events. Lauren was a knowledgeable and qualified partner for the endeavor, having lost her brother to addiction and experienced my sober journey firsthand. In fact, we dedicated this project to Chris as a way to honor his memory. The work was and still is very rewarding and fulfilling and gives me purpose.

I was also back on a hit show, entertaining millions and doing it next to my best friends. Life seemed to be perfect. Seriously, it felt like I was a character in my own fairy tale. All the hard work was finally being rewarded with smooth seas on the horizon.

Then, we got the greatest news of all: Lauren was pregnant! We had conceived on my first night home from prison. I don't know how to properly describe how happy we were. Overjoyed. It seemed as if everything we had gone through had led us here to this amazing moment.

But not long after, we were blindsided with disaster. Lauren had a miscarriage. Just like that, our first child was lost. Similar to how it was hard to put into words the elation we felt at learning we were pregnant, no description can properly emote the devastation we now felt. It was a sharp, indescribable pain for both of us, having this life taken before it ever had a chance. It was a gut punch I wasn't expecting, and frankly, one I didn't think we deserved.

This was different from the other adversities I'd overcome. This was harder. Prison—I could physically handle that. Addiction—it affected Lauren, no doubt, but it was my pain to shoulder. This wasn't like that. This was happening to my wife directly, and I would have done anything to take away her pain. I felt helpless but quickly turned that sentiment around. Having gone through so much crisis in my life, I instinctively went into crisis management mode. I knew exactly what to do to overcome this tragedy.

Ultimately, Lauren and I clung to our faith in God, faith in each other, and faith in ourselves. We dusted each other off and helped each other get back on our feet, recognizing that no matter what life throws at you, the only path is forward, one step at a time.

Being reality stars, we didn't try to hide what we were enduring. We allowed the loss of our pregnancy to be a part of the show, just like everything else in our life. I realized the importance of this moment, knowing that magnifying it could help other couples in the same situation. We struggled to find the silver lining in all of this, but if there was one, it was helping others. My job was to show the world what I was going through, and we made our loss a focal point during filming in the hope it would bring relief to others.

After a second miscarriage, we knew we had to do something. Both Lauren and I underwent physicals, and it was revealed that she was suffering from endometriosis. Honestly, it was a relief. This was an issue that we could work to solve. Like always, we wanted to focus on the solution rather than the problem. After all, God gives his toughest battles to his strongest soldiers.

Lauren's slight thyroid issue could be regulated with meds, while a relatively straightforward surgery through her belly button would clean the endometriosis out. The surgery was successful, and a few months later, we got wonderful news: we were pregnant again!

We were on a work trip in Vegas, shooting season three of *Family Vacation*, when we found out. We just so happened to have packed a pregnancy test, and after getting a positive result, we had a big conversation with the head producers, SallyAnn Salsano and Ashli Tortorello. We all knew this was a huge moment for the show. MTV really wanted to film it, but they also wanted to respect our wishes and feelings. Since we'd publicly been through those two previous miscarriages, they gave us the choice whether to film the news or not.

"We know this will get a lot of eyeballs, but if it's going to hurt you, we won't air it," they said. If we did film and things ended up not going our way, they offered to cut the footage and never air the storyline.

That was big to me. In all my time working with MTV, they had never before offered to cut something if we later didn't want to make it public. Part of being a reality star is showing the world everything that you're going through—the good, the bad, and the ugly. It meant a lot to us, but my default setting was positive vibes. Even though the pregnancy was new and we weren't in the "safe zone" when most people announce, I was all about manifesting the outcome you want and deserve. I was like, "Let's go with what's happening. Let's share our wonderful news with our friends and the world."

We only had to keep the secret for about ten days. On the last day of filming, while the cameras rolled, we let our castmates know we were expecting. They were shocked and overjoyed for us while probably a little nervous also. We were too, but focusing on a potential negative outcome was not my style. I choose to look at all the ways things can go right instead of how they can go wrong. It meant a lot to share this wonderful news with the people we were closest with while also demonstrating our resiliency to the world.

I'm happy to say the rest of the pregnancy went flawlessly. It was like we were finally living that elusive fairy tale. Of course, not everything could be peaches. This was during COVID lockdowns, so we spent most of that time at home enjoying our growing family, which was fine with me. I'd just done eight months locked down in prison; I could do a year or two at home with my wife and dog, no problem.

It was funny though—the state of New Jersey actually called me up and asked me to record the messages they sent to residents: "Two weeks to flatten the curve." (We all know how that worked out.) I was flattered and agreed to do it but had to laugh at the irony. *The government just sent me to prison; now, they want me to address the public on their behalf and tell them to stay home!*

Despite lockdowns and mask mandates, I still had my community service to do, and my probation officer made it clear that responsibility wasn't going away, even if everything was still shut down. It made me think of the saying, "Nobody cares—work harder."

"Cool," I said once I found out I was way behind on my hours. "I'll knock these out." Ultimately, I completed my five hundred hours within the two years allotted.

We celebrated each milestone of Lauren's pregnancy: The first prenatal appointment. The end of the first trimester. Hearing the heartbeat. Month seven hit, then month eight. Everything was going great. Finally, the ninth month arrived. The doctors decided to induce Lauren. Our bundle of joy was on his way.

May 25, 2021. It was 6:00 p.m., and MTV was downstairs waiting to take us to the hospital. The bags were packed, crib put together, and the house babyproofed. We were ready to bring our firstborn into the world, then take him home to our family's dream house.

Because of how much I'd endured in my life, I didn't let my guard down, remaining alert and focused. I wasn't naïve enough to think it would just be smooth sailing from here. I knew life happened on life's terms, so I stayed diligent, ready to put out a fire if one popped up. In my experience, something always happened; my concentration needed to stay on how I would handle it if and when it did.

Still, I remained cautiously optimistic as we checked into our suite at the hospital. Again, because MTV was filming, we received top-notch accommodations. They gave Lauren her induction medicine and the epidural, and everything was going great. I was in my glory, ordering Shake Shack, texting the squad, so excited to be a dad.

But Lauren's labor went slow. She wasn't dilatating as fast as they wanted. They had her do some exercises on a yoga ball to speed up the process, but it didn't seem to be working. All of a sudden, a doctor announced that the baby wasn't breathing or there was something wrong with his heartbeat. "Ah, hell no," I said. "I don't know what you guys are doing with that ball, but it's time to get this baby out!"

The doctors and nurses began to prep Lauren for surgery. After hours and hours of labor, my poor wife was exhausted, and now she would have to undergo a C-section. During the procedure, I was literally the most scared I had ever been in my life, terrified something else was going to go wrong.

I stood at her shoulder as the surgery commenced. Everything seemed to be moving in slow motion. Doctors and nurses moved around Lauren until suddenly, one announced, "Any minute now!" Then, it got silent. For a moment, I didn't hear anything. I felt lightheaded. I was like, *Oh my God, is the baby breathing?* Finally, after the longest few seconds of my life, the most beautiful cry I'd ever heard rang out like church bells. They handed me my baby son. I looked at Lauren, exhausted but smiling.

"We've done it, honeys," I said. "We made it." Even with everything, we had reached the finish line safe and sound. Welcome to the world, Romeo Reign Sorrentino, born May 26, 2021, at 6:32 p.m., coming in at six pounds, eight ounces, and nineteen inches long.

Drained but over the moon, our family of three hunkered down in our hospital suite, awaiting discharge. Over the next two days, friends and family came to visit and meet Romeo. The squad adorned the outside of our house and lawn with baby decorations. We'd been through the wringer but had made it. It was time to go home.

We finished packing. The car was ready downstairs. MTV was present to film our hospital exit and happy return home.

That's when the doctor came in.

"There's a problem with Romeo," he said sternly. "You're not going home."

CHAPTER 31

DREAMS INTO NIGHTMARES

It was as if my dreams had intersected with my nightmares. We tried to remain optimistic and positive, but there was no way around it. The devastating news that something was wrong with Romeo shattered the anticipation of a "normal" childbirth experience, abruptly blowing whatever expectations we held onto to bits. When there is something wrong with your child, the pain is unimaginable, and this was a new level of hurt. The only messaging the doctors gave us was, "His temperature is slightly elevated, and we can't send him home until we figure out why and fix it."

It felt like we were being kept in the dark, but the reality was they weren't able to diagnose what was wrong with Romeo. That might have been the scariest part—simply not knowing. Just like when Lauren miscarried, I felt helpless. I didn't know how to fix this. There was nothing I could do but be strong for my wife and make the best decisions for my son. Human nature meant my imagination and insecurities could get the best of me if I allowed them, so I pushed down all the surging emotions to remain the rock my family needed.

Romeo underwent test after test. Each day was filled with more and more. The good news was that each one came back negative. The bad news was his fever didn't relinquish. It meant his body was fighting something off, and they couldn't figure out what it was.

Every day was an escalation. The tests became more invasive. They wanted to do a spinal tap. Reluctantly, we consented. Their first attempt failed, and they had to do it a second time. The procedure ruled out both viral and bacterial meningitis, which was great, but it was a traumatic procedure during a traumatic time. We continued jumping through hoop after hoop as every possible illness was tested for and eliminated.

Finally, the hospital told us that Lauren needed to be discharged. They said they could only keep her for so long after a C-section, and that time was up. The last thing we wanted to do was leave our baby in the NICU without us, but there was no choice. We had to go home without our newborn son. My wife and I were drowning in a rising sea of despair.

I'll never forget that somber drive home from the hospital without our child. Lauren was inconsolable while I did everything in my power to keep from breaking down. This had become the toughest trial I'd ever faced. I believe that God had put those other battles in front of me to prepare me for this one.

We pulled up to the house and were greeted with a lawn and driveway full of well-meaning messages and signs from my *Jersey Shore* castmates in the colors of the Italian flag. "Welcome Home Baby Sitch" was spelled out cheerfully. The sentiment was heartfelt and appreciated, but the obvious issue was that Baby Sitch wasn't coming home.

When we got inside, both of our mothers were waiting for us. The new grandmas cried while trying to console Lauren. I remained steadfast, showing no emotion. The switch had been flipped to full crisis mode, and there was no time to be in my feelings.

Each day, Lauren and I drove home from visiting our son in the hospital, knowing an empty nursery and crib awaited us. I kept thinking how this wasn't the way it was supposed to be while Lauren sobbed in the passenger seat. We'd stop at a red light, and I'd have to force myself to hold it all in. My eyes may have welled up, but I refused to succumb to my anguish. I had to remain strong. It was a scary time, but I wouldn't allow myself to be scared. It went back to my philosophy of remaining positive and moving forward one step at a time.

The days went on, and they still couldn't find a cause for Romeo's fever. He was receiving intravenous antibiotics and meds to keep the fever down while the tests continued, but he couldn't go home until the fever dissipated or they found and cured the cause.

I didn't know this until I had a baby in the NICU, but a newborn's veins are very small, and it can be difficult to get a needle in. When such a tiny baby needs intravenous fluids for a prolonged period, the doctors and nurses often struggle to get a line in to administer medicine. This is what eventually happened with Romeo. The hospital staff had exhausted the veins in his arms, then his legs, and eventually had to put an IV in his head, just a horrible, upsetting sight. But soon, even that IV was no longer viable. The doctor came to me and explained that they'd run out of places to stick my son and he wanted to do surgery to implant a direct line. A tube would be implanted into a large vein in Romeo's chest.

I saw this as one of the biggest decisions of my life, one that required unsheathing my sword and shield. I started swinging.

"Absolutely not," I stated defiantly. "We are not going to do that to my son. Find a spot to put the IV. I don't care where it is. Foot, head, hand, just find a line. We're not doing surgery."

Ultimately, it was the right decision. Romeo had four days left to complete his cycle of antibiotics. After day fourteen and many, *many* prayers as we clung to our faith, the fever miraculously subsided. We had no way of knowing if it would come back or what the cause had been, but after undergoing a standard newborn hearing test, Romeo was discharged. We were going home. Finally, our family would be complete.

We alerted MTV that we would be leaving the hospital. They gathered a production crew and met us downstairs. We'd been through a lot in those two weeks but were finally ready to introduce the Sorrentinos, party of three, to the world.

This time, when we arrived home, only tears of happiness fell. Both our mothers were awaiting our arrival, this time bustling around the kitchen. Mama Peaches was doing her thing, and other family members came by to meet Romeo and drop off platters of food.

Once we settled in as a family, it was like the dream had finally been realized. All the hard work, all the setbacks, had led us to this wonderful place. Romeo was happy, healthy, and if anything, developing ahead of schedule. He was a tough little cookie, just like his dad.

I was over the moon about being a father. It's really all I ever wanted in life. With my past, it had been no guarantee. I'd had to fight tooth and nail to get here, but my dreams had come true. Lauren was naturally a wonderful mother. It was instinctive for her.

I loved every second of raising baby Romeo. I still do. I learned to change diapers, feed him, burp him. I took pride in all of it. I felt like we deserved this happiness, and I wanted to soak in each tiny aspect of fatherhood.

Like always, we did it all in front of the cameras, with full transparency to the world. I enjoy telling my story, and I wouldn't change a thing. I've parlayed my fifteen minutes of fame into fifteen years and counting. Now, America would get to watch the next generation of Situations on their television screens.

The ratings for *Jersey Shore: Family Vacation* stayed high while the show continued to be a staple for MTV as their number-one show on Thursday. Lauren and I loved our job filming and going on adventures with our closest friends. So did the audience. *Family Vacation* kept getting renewed, and along with it, we received new contracts. Soon, I was back at six figures per episode. We won Reality Show of the Year in 2020 and were also presented a lifetime achievement award from MTV as reality royalty. We finally got our popcorn trophy! I still smile each day as I walk past that iconic trophy exhibited proudly in my hallway.

My victory over addiction hit seven years in December of 2022. While thriving in sobriety, I continued consulting for treatment facilities and helping others find the peace I have been so fortunate to uncover. I opened up several other successful businesses, including a supplement company called Brotrition (I recommend the Funfetti-flavored whey protein). Lauren developed a skin care company called "Laurens," my nickname for her, that took off. We were living our best lives while teaching others to do the same.

In 2022, my voting rights were restored after the completion of probation and community service. Then, in August of 2023, the government issued me a new passport and removed my travel restrictions. Those were the culminating pieces of punishment from my tax conviction, marking the official end of that grievous mistake. I'm proud to say that stage of my life is now closed and solidly in the past.

Despite our happiness, we weren't immune from new pain. Life still had to run its course on its own terms. In 2022, our beloved golden retriever, Moses, was diagnosed with cancer. The vet told us it was a death sentence and that he wouldn't have more than a few weeks to live. We did everything we could, including surgery, chemotherapy, dietary supplements, and CBD, but after nine months of fighting, Mosey's quality of life had degraded enough that there was an emergency visit to the vet. There, the doctors informed us that Moses only had hours to live and that we had to make a tough decision to ease that transition. After spending ten years by my side, my best friend, Lauren's protector while I was in prison, and our biggest supporter through everything we'd been through, Moses Sorrentino passed. All good dogs go to heaven, of that, I'm sure.

But God gives when he takes away. Two weeks later, Lauren and Romeo came down the stairs. Lauren set the little guy on the floor. He had just learned to walk and waddled over to me like a drunk sailor, his smile big and infectious. When I reached down to pick my son up, I noticed writing on his shirt. "Big Bro" was written across it.

I looked at Lauren, and her face said it all. We were going to be parents again! It was as if new life had come from Moses's death.

This time around, we were ready for anything. They say experience is the best teacher, and we had plenty of that. There was still some scar tissue from the other pregnancies and Romeo's hospital stay, so part of us was waiting—and preparing—for the other shoe to drop. But this time around, everything went so smoothly it was almost unnerving. The pregnancy had no complications, and after nine thankfully uneventful months, the day was here—a planned C-section to deliver our daughter.

Like with so many major life milestones, an MTV camera crew waited for us downstairs to film our drive to the hospital. Later that day, on January 24, 2023, at 8:22 in the morning, Mia Bella Sorrentino came into the world, weighing five pounds, fifteen ounces, and measuring eighteen inches long. Honestly, we were somewhat in shock at the lack of difficulties—we were used to putting out fires! But it seemed as if God were saying, "You've already proven yourself. I got this one." Mia Bella's birth went perfectly, and we even took her home a day earlier than planned. Sorrentino, family of four!

We were living the American dream. I'd married my college sweetheart, a woman I loved with all my heart. We had two beautiful, healthy children. We lived in our dream home in the same town where my wife grew up. I had the best job in the world and an amazing story to go along with it. I got to watch my kids grow up, and they got to have a sober dad, a mindful dad, one who is present and loving.

Just the other day, as Laurens and I stood in the kitchen, I gave her a kiss and wrapped my arms around her lovingly. From the corner of my eye, I noticed Romeo watching. He clocked the biggest grin and ran to us at top speed. He'd just learned about group hugs and didn't want to miss out. As I felt his tiny arms stretching as wide as they could around our legs, I looked down at my daughter sleeping in a bassinet. A sense of serenity enveloped me. It occurred to me that life doesn't get any better than this. I couldn't think of a happier feeling for a human being. This was the real lotto-winning moment.

Lauren turned to me. "I think we might need a bigger house," she said jokingly.

I looked at her, eyes wide. "Huh?"

Her smile and glow said it all. "I'm pregnant," she confirmed.

My first reaction was, "Say again?" Once the news settled in, I was instantly overjoyed. We'd both always wanted three children. Our dreams continued to come true.

Then, it dawned on me. I didn't get what I prayed for until I became the person that should receive it.

I've walked through the fires and come out a better man. A family man. A good man. One I am proud of.

My story is crazy, I know that. Now, you do too. People stop me on the street and sometimes cry because they think they know what I've been through. But only after reading this book will they truly understand all the pain and sacrifice it's taken to get where I am today. My hope is that it shows them they can do the same. Often, people tell me that they or a loved one are going through something similar. Addiction. Loss of friends and family. Prison. A miscarriage. Things

I've experienced and come through stronger. I represent hope to those people, a weighty responsibility I take very seriously.

I know that my example can serve to help so many. My experiences prove that you can beat the disease of addiction and enjoy a happy, safe, and productive life. If you're struggling, know that I was there. For years, it seemed like there was no escape, no happy ending. But with the right mentality, hard work, and a refusal to quit, I promise you too can come out the other side.

But I don't look at my story as having a happy ending. Instead, it's a happy beginning. I have no idea what the next chapter will entail, but I know what it is called. The next chapter of my life is called...

Peace.

EPILOGUE

Mama Peaches stood over the stove, slowly stirring the Sunday Sauce as it simmered Sorrentino style. Water boiled in a large cast-iron pot, waiting for the raviolis to go in. Hand-rolled meatballs and sausages crackled on another burner while lightly fried chicken cutlets cooled on a plate on the counter. My mother surveyed it all, this momentous feast to mark the end of the terrible ordeal that nearly ripped our family apart.

The wide smile on her face was more of peace and relief than bliss. Her boys were out of prison, safe and sound under one roof. Finally, she could sleep at night. Marc had been released from prison early because of COVID. Now that we had both officially paid our debt to society, the whole family could move forward with their lives with heads held high. As Mama Peaches looked around the room at her family, tears of happiness dotted her face.

Melissa finished setting the table while my brother-in-law, Mike, sipped a Scotch in the living room. Lauren chatted quietly with Marc's fiancée, Nikki, on the couch. Frank handed me a glass of ice and a can of Diet Coke as Mom called us all to dinner. Everyone took their places in the dining room. All of us, as a family, breaking bread together for the first time in almost two years. It didn't get any better than this.

As we went around the room saying what we were grateful for, I couldn't help but observe the people I loved. When it was my turn, I commented on how thankful I was for my freedom and my family. I then smiled to myself and thought, *If only people knew what I'd had to go through in order to make it to this table...*

It would certainly make a hell of a story.